The Concept of Man in Non-Western Cultures

A Guide for One's Own Research

Handbook
to Lothar Käser's Textbook
Animism – A Cognitive Approach

Robert Badenberg

/VTR
Publications

Bibliographic Information Published by the Deutsche Nationalbibliothek
The Deutsche Nationalbibliothek lists this publication in the Deutsche
Nationalbibliografie; detailed bibliographic data are available in the Internet
at http://dnb.d-nb.de.

ISBN 978-3-95776-115-6

VTR Publications
Gogolstr. 33, 90475 Nürnberg, Germany, http://www.vtr-online.com

Translated from German
by Derek Cheeseman of MissionAssist (http://www.missionassist.org.uk)

Printed by Lightning Source

"Stammi" & Marco

Contents

Foreword

If you ask people with little or no awareness of a Christian cognitive framework what animism is, their only reaction is usually a shrug of the shoulders. By contrast people who are Christians usually produce a definitive catch phrase on the spot, namely: "Animism is belief in spirits!" In terms of getting to the heart of the matter this statement is hardly better than the shrug of the shoulders. In reality it contains no more truth than the assertion that the essence of being a Christian is the gift of speaking in tongues.

If animism were no more than belief in spirits then this definition would also be valid for Christianity, for the latter also believes in the reality of spirit beings. First and foremost there is the Holy Spirit, then there are angels, and hardly any Christian doubts the existence and reality of demons.

Hence equating animism with belief in spirits is a totally inadmissible simplification, at best a eurocentric version of the facts. Worse still, this simplification hampers our attempts to perceive animism in the way people do who live by it. Whatever we can perceive with the help of such simplifications is at most a caricature of what animism really is, i.e. a holistic concept of the cosmos including its visible and invisible inhabitants, containing – among many others – elements which are to be interpreted as spiritist and occult, and comprising a characteristic theory of the nature of both objects and people.

If we want to understand the animistic cognitive system we must focus particularly on its concept of man. Access to it can only be achieved by proceeding systematically. A basic prerequisite for this is knowledge of the language spoken by the people whose culture is shaped by such an animistic system of thought. Incidentally acquired knowledge is not enough to give the outsider, whether missionary, teacher, doctor or nurse, the necessary insights for operating effectively within a society governed by an animistic cognitive framework.

Robert Badenberg has created such an access. His handbook provides a catalogue of questions which enables one to carry out one's own investigations competently and without being side-tracked, leading to an effective understanding of the animistic concept of the world and of man in all its details.

Lothar Käser

Acknowledgments

This Handbook has a rather singular history. First, it was through the interaction I had with my friend and colleague Gerhard Stamm when he came for a visit to Zambia in May 2002 that the idea to set out and write about this subject was born. It was the exchange of experiences and ideas that intrigued me and set me on a course I would have otherwise delayed – maybe indefinitely. Therefore, I take this opportunity to thank him for hours of worthwhile time spent.

To begin with it was just thoughts and ideas which in the course of conversation seemed to me to have important application in researching the concept of man in unfamiliar cultures. However, it soon became apparent that such a project would have to be set out much more comprehensively than I at first assumed. The first flood of ideas led to an initial rough draft of the manuscript, which then remained on the back burner for a fairly long time.

Nevertheless the project was not totally forgotten – thank God. This was due to what I learned and experienced when working and living among people in the northern province of Zambia, all of which continually admonished me not to lose sight of the importance of this matter. In addition the curiosity of colleagues and their questions as to how I was getting on with putting pen to paper occasionally gave the project small boosts. Marco Vedder played a substantial part in these boosts, and I thank him warmly for it.

My involvement in the Bemba Bible Translation Project, with its main support base in Kasama where I and my family lived for many years, also contributed considerably to this work. This environment was virtually ideal for gaining a fresh perspective on the various topics and focusing on relevant questions. I owe special thanks to Dr. Ernst R. Wendland. As Translation Consultant of the United Bible Societies and the Bible Society of Zambia he encouraged me in the early stages to continue with this work, both through his interest in the project and his assessment that it could make a very useful contribution to the work of Bible translation.

Finally it was my own field research, begun a long time ago, that motivated me to continue working on the manuscript. In a first research study I had already concentrated on the Bemba concept of man, culminating in a Masters thesis with an anthropological and missiological orientation. Further studies as part of a doctoral programme enabled me to widen the field research. That which was taken fairly little account of in the Masters thesis – the Bemba notions of the body – was made good in the dissertation, as fitted the breadth of the topic.

Although my own investigations had produced results from the many years of questioning and researching, there was no handbook which would bring all this together for the benefit of those similarly interested in attempting to research the concept of man among the ethnic group where they worked.

One of the difficulties of the project was how to present the experiences and pro-cedures of these investigations in an orderly and systematic way. It was in this connection, when the manuscript was at an advanced stage that Lothar Käser's textbook *Animism* was of assistance. It already had the necessary classification. I thank him most warmly for this contribution and for the intensive mutual ex-changes during the various phases of writing.

I must also thank my friends to whom I was regularly able to refer my project. Although many of them found the various topics addressed singular and unfamil-iar they listened patiently to my oral observations.

If I add at this point my warm thanks to my wife Rita this is not because it is the custom to insert this into the acknowledgements. Her supports in listening, in discussing, in critical reading, above all her appreciation of this work, were in-valuable. I also thank my sons Ralph and Frank. They made sure that I was lured out of my study, which at times resembled a "cave" into which I had crawled in order to pose exotic questions, back into their world – and not only when I my-self felt it necessary.

I welcome with interest any feedback on projects investigating the concept of man in ethnic groups.

Ursheim, Spring 2013
Robert Badenberg

Introduction

"It is all so confusing"

As mentioned earlier it was the exchange of thoughts and ideas with Gerhard Stamm that enticed me to set out and dive into the project of writing this *Handbook*. In our conversations the topic of the nature of man – the issues of body, soul, and spirit – came up more "accidentally" than by deliberately focusing on this issue.

During the said visit (2002) he told me about his work in Papua New Guinea and in particular his assignments teaching Theology students. My interest was aroused. He then showed me some teaching material he had developed for a course called "Culture and Discipleship." One section of the course was entitled: *"The problem of understanding the nature of man."* In this section Gerhard tried to blend cultural and biblical concepts about the nature of man but could do so only sparingly. He said: "Here I got stuck. It is all so confusing." I know he is right! Evidently European-Western concepts, Simbu concepts (an ethnic group in the Highlands of Papua New Guinea with which he worked), and biblical concepts met head on.

I am thoroughly convinced that many missionaries have felt the same way as Gerhard. So did I! During my own time among the Bemba of Zambia I became more and more convinced that I needed a better understanding of their ideas on the nature of man. In order to advance beyond a 'here-I-got-stuck' situation on this subject, one has to adopt a better way of doing things. This understanding can be enhanced by ethno-linguistic research. One needs reliable data to work with and proper tools to do a good job.

While I was compiling a questionnaire prompted by my Papua New Guinea encounter, my former anthropology teacher and now colleague, Prof. Dr. Lothar Käser, was himself in the process of writing a *Textbook* on animism (Käser 2004). When he approached me to read through his manuscripts, it became evident that our individual work represented really complementary units and belonged together. His concern was more on the side of providing a textbook that would fundamentally deal with animism, where worldview and the nature of man are the central issues. He sought to offer data from cultures around the world to substantiate his findings, introduce students to unfamiliar concepts and life-styles, and create enough desire in people to go out there and discover for themselves the riches of such cultures.

Käser makes an emphatic plea that people working in foreign cultures need to take a keen interest in people's ideas on the nature of man. He repeatedly states that with regard to certain anthropological themes there exists only vague information due to the lack of reliable data. That is where this handbook comes in. Before embarking on a discovery tour one needs equipment and tools. The handbook follows up on issues raised in the textbook and seeks to put a tool into the hands of inquisitive minds. It is intended to help people to be at ease in case they get stuck, or are about to get stuck, whether in the collision of cultural concepts or when it comes to do the actual work.

Why a textbook and a handbook on the same topics? A textbook aims to set out the basic *subject matter* and deal with fundamental *questions*, whereas a handbook is intended to provide the necessary *qualitative and quantitative research material*, the results of which can form the content of a textbook. Since in this case the textbook already exists, this handbook aims to respond to the repeated insistence in the textbook that certain areas have received little, inadequate, or indeed hardly any research at all. It is my intention to focus on meeting these demands. This method of proceeding has resulted in an intentional reliance on the textbook for the structure and arrangement of this book.

If *you yourself* want to embark on a "research expedition" you need the appropriate equipment. That is the aim and purpose of this book. The confusion engendered in us when one's own and unfamiliar concepts confront each other in the encounter with other cultures may well be resolved or at least disentangled by practical support. The book shows ways of carrying out one's own investigations in an unfamiliar culture. In the subtitle I have deliberately avoided the term "field research". It could possibly deter those who do not wish to regard themselves as "researchers" or cannot do so because of their particular sphere of work.

I have found that the need for such a handbook is confirmed by the experiences and accounts of missionaries and church workers – and professional anthropologists – serving in an unfamiliar cultural environment. During my own period as a missionary in Zambia I was always striving to learn from the people I was working amongst. I found that the lack of a suitable tool was a great impediment. Drawing on cognitive anthropology started a process of learning which opened up for me access to hitherto unknown worlds. Missionaries are incredibly privileged in getting to know other ways of living in our world (cf. Käser 2014:38). Hence they should never dismiss lightly, let alone treat as unwelcome ballast the opportunities offered to them. In my opinion such recognition is reason enough to offer practical support in a systematic way. Missionaries and church workers are going to people who, just like themselves, are shaped by their physical, geographical and cultural world. In the context of this intercultural encounter one can therefore not afford to attach less significance to the cognitive framework of the culture in which one is living and working.

A Universal Cultural Issue

All cultures are interested in enquiring about *the nature of man* and *what it means to be a human being*. For many cultures this question is not a peripheral issue but lies at the centre of their concept of the world, for concepts of the world shaped by animism each reveal at their centre their own characteristic concept of man (Käser 2014:38). Hence it is worth emphasising again here that investigating an ethnic group's concept of man is a priority in getting to know the cognitive model of another culture.

This requires a lot more than just scratching at the surface. You can only really "dig" into it by drawing systematically on the language of the host culture. In many parts of the world trade languages (*lingua franca*) have developed over time, partly linking even several countries or hundreds of different ethnic groups (e.g. Swahili in East Africa or Pidgin English in Papua New Guinea). These languages have only a limited suitability for investigating the concept of man of a particular ethnic group. On the one hand the vocabulary is rather limited, and on the other, many speakers of a trade language have grown up with their own mother tongue. This means that the process of enculturation – and the inherent cognitive model allied to it – have taken place in a language which in many cases is very different from the respective trade language.

One should therefore aim at carrying out the investigations in the language of one's informants. The language that people learn first, and which they use inside the social group where they live, is the language in which their cognitive model and thought categories about their cultural world are stored in the brain and are emotionally rooted in the psyche. The emotional component of a language must not be underestimated. Situations which persons finds extremely difficult to cope with and demand very much from them emotionally are approached inwardly in the thought patterns which permit them to give expression to their feelings and emotions. This succeeds best in their mother tongue

Any investigation of the concept of man held by an ethnic group must cover five big areas: *notions of the body*, the *seat* of the *emotions*, *intellect* and *character* or *personality features*, and *notions of the existence of the person after the death of the body*. I deliberately intend *not* to use the terms 'soul' and 'spirit', for they impede research rather than provide it with any benefit.[1] It is precisely at this point that blurring and complications arise in many ethnographies. In addition these areas present a big challenge in the work of Bible translation.

In his book *Anthropology of the Old Testament* (1984) Hans Walter Wolff has shown convincingly how great and serious the deficiencies are when important key anthropological terms are imprecisely translated by 'heart', 'soul', 'flesh', and 'spirit'.[2]

According to Wolff this resulted in misunderstandings which were not without consequences. Worth mentioning in the first instance would be the bi-partite and tri-partite concept of man derived from the Septuagint, the Greek translation of the Old Testament. This concept of man established body, soul and spirit as the three constituent parts of man. Furthermore it is claimed that it is possible to separate them entirely from each other and let them appear in stark contrast to each other (1984:21). Semitic concepts were partly overlaid by Greek philosophy. The anthropology of the Old Testament texts, however, stands significantly apart from this Greek influence. The biblical witness of the Old Testament dem-

---

[1] This also applies to a whole string of other ethnological terms such as 'main soul', 'organ soul' or 'body soul', 'shadow soul', 'image soul', 'free soul', 'journey soul', etc.

[2] See also Baker 2003.

onstrates clearly that man does not *have* a 'body', 'soul' and 'spirit' but *is* 'body', 'soul' and 'spirit'. (1984:26).

If the European-Western and Semitic concepts already produce such blatant discrepancies it is no wonder if field research in ethnic cultures which are not part of the five great religious traditions (Judaism, Christianity, Buddhism, Hinduism and Islam) is similarly complex and complicated – and probably more so. Since thought structures and concepts are concealed in the human brain, researching them requires detailed work.

It must be stressed again that the concept of man is a vital and central theme, both in the Bible and in serving in an intercultural environment. Gerhard Stamm's situation shows very clearly that time spent in field research is not a luxury, nor is it wasted and "unproductive". Rather the opposite is true! Insight and recognition developing out of a learning process produce good data (and better understanding!) and promote the respect of the local people. Such an atmosphere frequently results in good opportunities for real co-operation. Hence the question is:

How to succeed in getting behind the curtain?

Research into an ethnic group's concept of man is of the utmost importance. As already emphasised, the English terms (and also other Indo-Germanic ones) should be avoided as far as possible, indeed best altogether. It is essential to discover the structure of the indigenous concepts, for they are the key to the inner logic of how things relate. A good starting-point is to investigate the *notions of the body*. These constitute that area of the concept of man which (although largely ignored in research) is normally the most accessible, for it has to do with visible and tangible language material rather than with abstract linguistic concepts.

The facts and circumstances surrounding the research into an ethnic group's *notions of the soul* are rather different. This sphere of research requires careful language study, on account of the abstract patterns of thought. In this topic area European-Western notions of the soul contain features which are both immanent (of this world) and transcendent (of the beyond). This does *not* apply to cultures shaped by the phenomenon of animism. The 'soul' is a physical entity of this world; it is a concept closely combined with the body. Hence a better working concept for investigations in this area is the term *psyche*[3] or, as will be explained in detail later, the acronym *SEIC* (*Seat of the Emotions, Intellect and Character*).

---

[3] As an example, the White Fathers Bemba-English Dictionary s.v. *-lingana*. In context this verb can be used in *Imitima ya bantu tailingana*. The English translation given is: "the souls of men are not alike, do not resemble each other." But what is actually meant relates to the differences in a person's thinking, feeling and disposition, i.e. which are not conterminous. This is what the word means *(imitima – hearts)*. Clearly the text refers to living persons. The non-conterminous *imitima* are to be traced back to each individual (*SEIC*).

The issue is similar with the term 'spirit'. In European-Western notions this topic area also has natural and supernatural dimensions. The semantic field of the term 'spirit' has many layers. Traditional cultures focus much more on the development of concrete notions of the person and the continuation of the personality after the death of the body. Hence it is always to be used in the context of *the being which survives the death of the body* and *carries forward the personality of the deceased person*.

I am deliberately avoiding long explanatory passages and detailed references to the relevant literature such as might be expected in a scholarly publication. It seems to me that it is more important to offer this book to interested researchers as a modest helping hand in their field investigations.

The Target Readership

It is very clear to me that this handbook is a select rather than a general instrument, for it investigates a quite special sphere of interest, both in the area of missiology and in anthropology. Its selectivity is therefore necessary. For this reason it aims to gain the attention of *mission personnel* who teach mission courses in an intercultural context or as an integral part of medical work. In addition it has practical application for *Bible translation teams* and *professional anthropologists.*

I know from my own experience how difficult some of the tasks are that a good Bible translation has to resolve, whether they concern particularly those anthropological key terms 'soul', 'spirit', 'heart' or those many others which in my view can only be conveyed from one language (the source text may be Hebrew and Greek, or an English version) into another with great care and attention. All those working (or who have worked) on such projects will surely confirm this.

I very much hope that this handbook will succeed in deepening or indeed initially awakening an interest in the topic of the concept of man among many interested "researchers". I believe especially that mission personnel in particular should study it in more detail. Although it involves intensive work the journey of discovery in other cultures brings much reward: you learn the language of the host culture and gain more assurance and competence in handling this whole matter of culture. There are certainly missionaries who could have moved beyond the status quo so far reached – taking the gospel with them – if they had only been more seriously encouraged and been provided with practical support.

And there is more: data which is collected with method and system will help to provide an established and reliable data bank from cultures from all over the world and so widen our horizons significantly. Moreover mission personnel will have increased opportunity to draw on global knowledge more efficiently, and this above all *"for the sake of doing the missionary task well and making the Christian approach an intelligent, constructive one"*, as Hendrik Kraemer put it almost sixty years ago (1947:341).

Addenda in the form of helps and examples such as those in chapter 4 are there for reference or as examples of the difficulties that Bible translation has to reckon with.

The appendices set out the important key terms relevant to the Chuuk culture (Micronesia) and the Bemba culture (Zambia – Southern Africa). These should further indicate the purpose of one's own investigations in seeking to understand the concept of man of a particular culture, and also make a contribution to comparative studies – one of the strengths of anthropology!

Chapter 1
The Human Body

This chapter deals with the human body. It explains how a range of questions pertaining to the human body can be structured. The aim is to establish and analyse the notions of the anatomy and physiology of man as well as the functions of the organs of the body through linguistic research. Central to this approach is the anatomical vocabulary of the body, its internal and external organs, the semantic fields relating to the terms for the senses, how their functions are understood, and what the range of vocabulary – including idioms – concerning the body sensations is.

1.0 Introduction

Researching the concept of man can be conducted by employing a variety of guiding principles. For example, one may stress man's place within the universe, society, state, or family. Viewed from a different angle, one might focus on the meaning of life or man's duty to live a responsible life. However, these approaches may nevertheless fail to shed light on the true nature of man (Käser 2014:40).

The being of man contains first of all a very concrete fixed point – the *anatomy* and *physiology* of his body! Concepts of man must include as a central factor an ethnic group's notions of the human body. Käser even asserts that they are "indispensable for understanding animistic concepts of man" (2014:145). In practical terms this means that any research into a concept of man must begin with investigating the notions about the body.

With regard to Oceania Barthel has demanded that in dealing with the concept of the body one should not be satisfied with relying on just the lexical material but analyse indigenous texts by means of "a truly comprehensive and critically deepening study". In his view it would be important also to understand "all semasiological nuances (including mood content and ancillary meanings) **in the medium of the language itself.**"[4] Furthermore "a technique for collecting and ordering material would proceed according to the rules of onomasiology.[5] This would apply to constructing particular word groups (e.g. **parts of the body**)" (in Käser 2014:52).

A method of procedure such as Barthel demands for Oceania is also of fundamental validity for other areas. It is the aim of this chapter to provide such a "technique of data gathering and classification". The advantage this offers when beginning with the human body is immediately apparent:

---

[4] Semasiology is the science of the meanings of words in a given language.

[5] The branch of linguistics that deals with concepts and the terms that represent them, in particular contrasting terms for similar concepts, as in a thesaurus. http://www.oxforddictio naries.com/definition/english/onomasiology (24 March 2014).

First, the researcher and his informant(s) share something very basic in common: the human body. Although there may be differences in the outward appearance they are more or less trivial in comparison with the commonalities. Right from the start there is a lot of common language material.

Second – and this is a positive factor for the researcher – almost every member of any particular culture can make contributions here and be asked about the body and its conditions. Concepts of man are not just made up of abstract features. There are quite elementary things which are of first importance, such as how people in any society understand their physicality, how they talk about the body (comprehend it linguistically and conceptually) and what notions about it are current.

Here it is important (as indeed in all cases) to put questions in the language of the informants. If you have to work with interpreters it is best if the language is their mother tongue. In addition they should be fairly fluent in the researcher's own language. This first section discusses those questions which are important and which ones can be asked.[6]

In appropriate places this chapter and those which follow will regularly point to examples resulting from my own research among the Bemba in the north of Zambia.

---

[6] For case studies on this topic the works of Käser (1989) and Badenberg (2008) can be consulted.

1.1   The Word for Body

1.1.1   What is the word for the human *Body*?

❑ **Important:**

Already at this early stage of the research one might be in for a big sur-
prise. It could be that in the receptor language there is no word for body.
That is to say, there is but ***ONE word for body and person!***

For example, some Native American Indian groups (like the Wintu of
North California) have in their language ***no*** word for body! Instead, they
always use and speak of the ***whole person***: *kot Wintu* (Lee 1959:133-
134).

Consequently there are also ***no specific terms for the parts of the body***;
body parts "are aspects or locations" of the body (1953:134).

In such a case, one must ask about for the ***condition*** of a particular aspect
or location in or on the body.

For example, 'a broken arm' becomes 'arm-broke-I', or in other words: *I-
the-broken-arm*. Emphasis is on the ***whole person*** with special emphasis
on a particular ***condition*** the person is experiencing, or a particular location in or on the body which has undergone a change.

Additional reading: **Badenberg** 2008, Chap. 3.

However, such a situation as prevails among the Wintu Indians seems to be the
exception. It is very likely you will discover at least one term covering the body.

After the establishment of the terminology that deals with the body, ask now for
the word that designates body parts. In African (Bantu) languages be aware of
passive noun constructions for body parts (see Example)!

⇨ **Example:**

In Bemba [a major Bantu language widely spoken in Zambia and the
southern part of the Democratic Republic of Congo] the word for body
parts is either *ifilundwa* or *ifipande*. The noun *ifilundwa* is derived from
the transitive[7] verb *ukulunda,* meaning *to add, to join onto.*

Ifilundwa with the verb stem *-lunda* and the passive suffix *-wa* is liter-
ally: the add-ons, the attached *'things'.*

The body (*umubili*) is therefore the sum total of all "add-ons", all "attached *things*".

---

[7] Transitive verbs are verbs that "denote an action which necessarily affects or passes over
to some person or thing other than the subject of the verb" (Nunn 1973: 6).

1.1.2   Is the word designating the human body also the term that designates the body of animals, birds or fish?

❑ **Important**

Does the term for body *only* apply to living beings?

1.1.3   Is the word for body applied to only those animals which fall into the category of "living beings"?

    a.   What is the term for living beings?

    b.   What are the characteristics of a living being?

☞ **Hint:**

It could be worthwhile to compile a data bank of all animals that are classified as living beings.

1.1.4   Does the term for body also apply to plants and trees?

1.1.5   If so, which plants and trees are they?

☞ **Hint:**

Make sure to collect the indigenous words. However, it could be of interest to design a data bank with the indigenous terms matching the scientific terms.

1.1.6   Does the word for body cover the whole body or is it strictly speaking the word for trunk only, excluding the limbs?

1.1.7   Does the word also designate the upper part of the body?

1.1.8   Does the word for body also stand for the person itself or mean the self of a person?

⇨ **Example:**

The Islanders of Chuuk say:
aa ekiyekiiy feyiyéchún wóón inisin chék
(he only thinks of his *inisin*/body = thinks only of himself, is ego-centric).
(Käser 1989).

☞ **Hint:**

It is advisable to collect as many contexts as possible in which the word for body appears. Informants ought to be indigenous speakers of the language.

1.1.9 Is the word for body also used in an *abstract sense*?

For example, in English there are a number of abstract usages such as: "the social body", "a corporate body", "the body of a motor-car", "the body of a concert hall", "a lake is a large body of water", "the heavenly bodies (the sun, moon and stars)", "the foreign body in the eye", etc.

Collect as many expressions as possible in which the vernacular word for body is used. *Idioms*, *Proverbs* or *Songs* (folk songs etc.) provide a rich source of discoveries.

❑ **Important:**

This approach will help to bring to light the whole range of meanings of a certain word. The proper term for this kind of linguistic work is "establishment of a domain".

As a rule of thumb ask *three* questions:

1. What is the respective body part called?

   Result: One gets a word.

2. What else does this word mean?

   Result: One gets (ideally) all situations in which this word plays a role or to which this word is applied.

3. What kind of body part is meant?

   Result: One gets the term that heads a certain domain of terms.

   Additional reading: **Käser** *Foreign Cultures*, Chap. 19.

1.1.10 What are the categories into which the human body is divided up? What are the linguistic terms for the sub-divisions of the human body?

⇨ **Example:**

The Islanders of Chuuk perceive the human body as being divided up into five parts: head, neck, trunk, arms and legs.

With the Bemba in Zambia, the human body is divided up into more distinguishable parts or areas: head, neck, shoulders and arms, breast, abdomen, back, hips, legs.

Additional reading: **Käser** 1989. **Badenberg** 2003 and 2008.

☞ **Hint:**

Essential in establishing the concept of body of a certain ethnic group is the inclusion of following areas: the act of breathing, heart- and blood circulation, digestion of food, the function of the spinal marrow, the genitals, conception, pregnancy, birth.

The thicker the description the better detailed statements on the concept of body can be made.

1.1.11 What are the words for *corpse or dead* body?

a. Is this word also the word for the dead body of an animal, a bird, of fish or insects?

☞ **Hint:**

In English one differentiates between a corpse (a dead body especially of a human being) and a carcass (a dead body of an animal).

b. Is this word for corpse or dead body a generic term, that is, does this word cover the corpse of a man, a woman or a child?

c. If not, what are the others words?

d. Is the dead body of an animal differentiated in terms of gender? Are there different words for the carcass of a male and the carcass of a female animal?

e. What is the word for "to die" or "dying"?

☞ **Hint:**

It is advisable to collect as many contexts as possible in which the word for body appears. Informants ought to be indigenous speakers of the language.

How do people say: "he/she is on the brink of death", "he/she gave up the ghost", "he/she breathed his/her last", "to die in one's bed", "to die in harness", "to die gamely", etc.

f. What is the word for death?

☞ **Hint:**

In many languages the word for death is rather short. For example: in German (*Tod*); in Danish (*død*); in Swedish (*död*); in Africaans (*dood*); in Bemba (*imfwa*); in Karanga (*rufu*); in Zulu (*isifo*); in Chuukese (*má*); in Tibetian (*'chi ba*); in Hebrew (*mot*) etc.

1.1.12 Is a corpse perceived as a "thing" or as "waste"?

☞ **Hint:**

The Bemba word for the dead body of a human being is *citumbi*. The prefix *(i)ci* is indicative of the word class for things or objects (*ici-ntu* = a thing or an object). However, if the prefix *-ci* or *ici* is affixed to a word stem that designates a living being (human) a derogative meaning is expressed.

First Example:

The word for man or male in Bemba is *mu-aume* = *mwaume* (sing.).

With the prefix *-ci* (word class of things or objects) one can form the word *ci-aume* = *caume*. *Caume* is extremely insulting and expresses contempt and despise. It means: "male brute".

Second Example:

An elderly person is called *mukote*. With the prefix *-ci* one can change the word *mukote* into *cikote* which is abusive language, e.g.: *we cikote we!* = "oh, you repulsive, repugnant old fool".

1.2   The External Body Parts or Body Areas

1.2.1   What are the most important *external body parts*?

a. Create questionnaires asking for words denoting the external body parts and build up a data bank or design a spread sheet and fill it with all the vernacular vocabulary gathered. That can be helpful in sorting words in different ways.

b. As the collection of words expands one should try to find out into which domains the bulk of words can be sorted. In other words, certain body parts might be grouped together forming a distinctive group under one heading.

This kind of structuring is called *establishing a taxonomy* of the human body.

⇨ **Example:**

Ask which body parts – *according to the understanding/ classification of the informant/s* – are part of the head, the trunk etc.

c. Continue working in this manner and group all body parts into their respective domains. With time the data bank will expand considerably and with it the taxonomy of the body according to the thought patterns and the linguistic structure of the people will emerge more clearly.

Additional reading: **Badenberg** 2008, Chap. 3.

❑ **Important:**

Establish the anatomy of a human being according to the linguistic domain of indigenous words and their respective meanings. European-Western concepts of body and the medical, scientific concept of man may in one way or another divert significantly from it.

It may help to use a picture or an anatomical image of a human body in order to speed up the inquiry. It will be possible to point out the exact part of the body and note the word or phrase in the vernacular. This may be helpful since one can avoid to pin-pointing each and every body part on a living person. It may also save one from possible embarrassment.

Particular body parts, for which there is no indigenous word or phrase, are often thought to belong to some other part of the body. Sometimes there is *no* word for a certain body part at all. This could be of interest and it is worthwhile to take particular note of it.

1.2.2 **Are certain body parts regarded as "good" or "important"?**

    a. What body parts are they? (Careful research is highly recommended!)

    b. What are the reasons why these body parts are regarded as "good" or "important"?

    c. What are the "most important" body parts?

1.2.3 **Are certain body parts regarded as "bad", "less attractive" or "less important"?**

    a. What body parts are they? (Careful research is highly recommended!)

    b. What are the reasons why these body parts are regarded as "bad", "less attractive" or "less important"?

1.3   The Internal Body Organs

1.3.1 **What are the terms for (all) *internal body parts*?**

☞ **Hint:**

It is advisable to begin with the major organs (heart, lungs, liver, stomach, kidneys etc.)

a. What is the word for heart?

b. What is the word for lung or lungs?

c. What is the word for liver?

d. What is the word for bile?

e. What is the word for kidney/kidneys?

f. What is the word for bladder?

g. What is the word for spleen?

h. Expand on the data bank by collecting (all) words designating other organs and internal body parts. It is advisable to note the organ or the body part and their respective functions. A list including the English, French, Spanish etc. equivalents as well as the proper medical terms may be of worth.

i. The ideas and explanations to do with the breathing system and what organs are parts of that system (e.g. what roles do the lungs or does the heart play) might be of special interest. Ideas on how the breath works its way through the body and how it keeps the body alive might diverge significantly from western or medical explanations.

See **Käser** *Animism*, Chap. 10.

1.3.2 What is the word for breath?

1.3.3 What is the word for breathing?

1.3.4 How is the act of breathing perceived, that is, how do people describe the act of breathing?

1.3.5 What role do the lungs play in the act of breathing?

1.3.6 What organs are involved in the act of breathing? Through which organs does the air pass in the act of breathing?

1.3.7 What relationship exists between the breath and the heart?

1.3.8 What is the word for stomach?

1.3.9 How is the act of digestion described, that is, how do people explain how food is digested?

See **Badenberg** 2008, Chap. 3.

1.3.10 What is the word for blood?

1.3.11 Is there a word for nerves?

1.3.12 Is there a word for brain?

    a. What functions does the brain carry out?

    b. Is there linguistic evidence that intellectual processes are associated with the brain?

       ☞ **Hint:**

       It is advisable to collect as many contexts as possible in which the brain is associated with intellectual processes. Informants ought to be indigenous speakers of the language.

1.3.13 Is the word for hair a generic term? Does it cover all kinds of hair on the (human) body?

    a. What is the word for hair (on the head)?

    b. What is the expression for "grey hair"?

    c. What are the words for "eye-brow/s", "moustache", "beard"?

    d. What are the words for hair on other body parts?

1.4   The Terms for the Senses

1.4.1 What are the words for the *senses* (sight, hearing, smell, taste and touch)?

    a. When asking for the words designating the senses, be sure to collect words in context. Always ask for complete sentences for each word covering the senses. One sentence for each single word designating one of the senses might not be enough. A collections of contexts in which the words for the senses appear should be attempted.

    b. ***Reckon with surprises!*** It may well be that informants will not be able to provide a separate word for each of the five senses! Some languages do not have words for all the senses. And other languages may have only one word for two or even three senses!

       ⇨ **Example:**

       In Bemba the word *ukumfwa* covers **three** senses: ***hearing, taste, and touch!***

c. This example illustrates the need for research. Only then can the us-age and the wide range of meanings of this word be established. Therefore – collect, collect, collect!

d. It might be of interest to find out whether some senses take prece-dence over others or if one sense might receive prime attention in comparison with the other senses.

e. If so, are there reasons for this preference? What are the individual opinions and what are the commonly shared views?

1.5   The Body Sensations

1.5.1 What is the word for *body sensations*?

a. Is there a term that heads a domain that covers all body sensations?

☞ **Hint:**

In case it is difficult to ask for this specific term right away, one might start by asking specific questions instead.

b. Use whole sentences to ask how to say:

- I feel cold
- I feel warm
- I feel pain (shoulder, arm, leg etc.)
- I have a (bad) headache / I suffer from headache(s)
- I am hungry/I feel hunger
- I am thirsty/I feel thirst
- I feel tired, feel fatigue
- I feel refreshed
- I am in a feverish condition
- What is the word for the sensation one feels when stroking the skin?

c. Having collected a large number of words – and especially phrases and idioms – which denote such feelings, one can now try to find the major term that covers all feelings pertaining to that category. Most likely there will be a term meaning something like: The *"feelings [sensations] of the body"*.

⇨ **Example:**

The Bemba language provides two terms which denote body sensations: The nouns are *imyumfwile* or *imyumfwikile* [derived from the verb *ukumfwa*: *the feelings*].

These two terms come with an extension: *imyumfwile/imyumfwikile ya mubili*, which mean the *feelings of the body,* that is, the body sensations.

This is indicative of the fact that there is one category of feelings that covers the whole body or feelings that can be felt on the whole body, and there is, however, also a second category of feelings which can only be felt at one location only!

d. In a next step one can now begin to put all other feelings which are not "feelings of the body" into a second group.

Again it is important not only to collect words alone but also to gather whole phrases or idioms. This work will be most important for the following chapter when emotions come into focus.

In all probability the term for *feelings is* also used in connection with the **heart** or with **another important organ** (most likely a major internal organ)!

⇨ **Example:**

As explained earlier, in Bemba there are two terms that denote feelings: *imyumfwile* or *imyumfwikile*.

Furthermore, *imyumfwikile* can carry the extension *ya mubili which* then specifically means the **"feelings of the body".**

In contrast, the phrase *imyumfwile/imyumfwikile* with the extension *ya mutima* speaks of the **"feelings of the heart"**, that is to say, the emotions, or in other words, the temporary psychical dispositions.

The *imyumfwikile ya mutima* are feelings that can only be felt at that one particular location!

Chapter 2
The *Seat* of *Emotions*, *Intellect* and *Character* Attributes *(SEIC)*

This chapter is meant to help investigate how in mainly oral societies the *Seat* of *Emotions*, of the *Intellect*, and the *Character* attributes (*SEIC*) can be determined and located. Furthermore, it will become clear why the euroamerican term "soul" is of little use in doing this kind of research.

2.0   Introduction

The previous chapter dealt with the ideas and beliefs people might have concerning the anatomy and the physiology of the human body. This chapter expands on the concept of man inasmuch as **three** more important areas of research come into focus. These areas are: the **Seat** of **Emotions**, of the **Intellect,** and the **Character attributes**. These three terms will from now on be referred to as the *SEIC*, an acronym that was first coined by Lothar Käser.[8]

This place, the *SEIC* of a person, needs to be determined through linguistic research. This chapter shows how a step-by-step research can be structured and should begin with the *Seat of Emotions*.

2.1   The Seat of Emotions

2.1.1   *Where* does one feel *emotions*?

   a. Ask for the words or phrases for love, hate, pity, joy, sorrows, to be downcast, to be devastated, to have lost all sense of hope, to feel forsaken, to be confident, to be hopeful, to feel happy, to be filled with joy, to feel gratitude, to feel honoured, to feel disgust and contempt, to feel fear, to be in anguish, to be nervous, to feel envy, jealousy, shame, honour, pride, remorse, greed, peace, to feel meek, to feel worthless, to feel sexually aroused, to feel being let down by others, to feel being treated injustly etc.

   b. Ask where those feelings manifest themselves or what part of the body is affected.

   c. Are those feelings associated with a certain *body organ* or a certain *part of the body*?

---

[8] This acronym was first introduced by Käser in *Animism* (2004/2014), especially chapter 10.

⇨ **Example:**

The heart	(Indo-Germanic languages)
The liver	(Indian languages in North- and South America)
The spleen	(African Pygmies)
The kidneys	(Old Testament)
The larynx	(Islanders of Belau)

Bantu ethnic groups in southern Africa or ethnic groups in Micronesia point at the chest or the region below the sternum. No particular internal organ is prominent.

Other ethnic groups believe the *diaphragm* or the *stomach* proper to be the place where the seat of emotions is localized.

Furthermore, there might well be a number of terms all of which denote the seat of emotions.

⇨ **Example:**

The Bemba language knows of three terms which relate to feelings and emotions. They are localized:

mu cifuba   in the ***chest***

mu nda   in the ***stomach***, inside the ***innermost*** or

mu mutima   in the ***heart***

Additional reading: **Badenberg** 2008, Chap. 3.

☞ **Hint:**

See Appendices 1 and 2!

d. Find out what kind of word it is (noun, verb) and if it carries or even requires certain prepositions.

⇨ **Example:**

The Bemba word *umutima (**heart**)* is a noun. In conjunction with the preposition of place ***mu*** one gets: *mu mutima* = in/inside the heart.

The preposition of place ***mu*** makes the heart appear with a chamber inside. Other prepositions might cause the heart to appear with an ***outside*** or to possess a certain ***form*** (large, small, wide, narrow, flat or rounded etc.). These prepositions do, however, first and foremost speak of the heart as the seat of emotions rather than its anatomical features.

The Bemba language has three prepositions of place which are used in conjunction with the word *umutima*.

Mu mutima speaks of what is going on __in__ the heart, that is, the feelings and emotions inside; the feelings and emotions a person has.

Ku mutima speaks of a direction or a movement __towards__ the heart. This implies things or events that move towards the heart and cause a person to develop certain feelings and emotions inside the heart. *Ku mutima* are things and events of external origin moving towards the heart and eventually affecting the heart inside.

Pa mutima describes a certain __condition__ of the heart. But often it is used as a euphemism for sicknesses or ailments involving the intestines (e.g. diarrhoea).

☞ **Important:**

Body sensations can be felt on the *whole* or *entire* body. But feelings and emotions are restricted to *one* location *only* which very often is an *internal* organ. Even if there are more terms which designate that one location or spot where feelings and emotions are manifest, they merely highlight different aspects of that place or organ.

This location or organ blends partly with what we call soul. But only partly and in insufficient manner! In order to avoid the very ambiguous word "soul" entirely, it is better to use and work with the acronym *SEIC*.

The Appendices 1 & 2 may serve as guiding examples. They show how these things relate to the Bemba (Africa) and the Chuuk (Micronesia) situation.

Appendix 3 contains a comparison between Bemba, German and Hebrew "soul" vocabulary.

Chapter 4 deals with the extensive domain of the Hebrew word *nefesh* that is often (and wrongly!) translated as "soul".

2.1.2   Collect as many terms as possible describing *feelings* and *emotions*!

a. As a guide: Design a spread sheet that contains the words of feelings and emotions in your own mother tongue.

b. Separate those feelings and emotions into good (positive) and bad (negative) ones and sort them accordingly.

c. As a guide: Describe situations in which one has such and such a feeling. Then, ask your informants for the word in their own language. Remember to collect whole sentences and expressions.

d. As the data bank grows over time, it will be possible to establish the main term denoting feelings and emotions.

As a rule of thumb ask *three* questions:

1. <u>What is the respective emotion called?</u>

Result: One gets a certain word.

2. <u>What else does this word mean?</u>

Result: One gets (ideally) all situations in which this word plays a role or to which this emotion is applied.

3. <u>What kind of emotion is it?</u>

Result: One gets the term that heads a certain domain of terms.

Keep two separate data banks of the indigenous words which contain the positive and negative feelings and emotions respectively.

☞ **Important:**

In general it is good to ask the informants in *which situation* they would have a *certain feeling* or would cause them to feel in a certain way. This will help to determine if a certain feeling is either positive or negative.

Promising sources of linguistic material are sermons, letters or oral accounts of indigenous persons in which they talk about their experiences and their inner life.

As the data bank expands one can begin to sort the kind of negative and positive feelings and emotions. One obvious marker of the bulk of words will be their metaphorical features.

Metaphor is a compound Greek word (*meta* = "from one to another" and *phero* = "I carry"). A metaphor is therefore *"the transference of a word properly referring to one set of objects to another set of objects"* (Nunn 1973:xii).

The metaphorical use of words is often more important than their plain usage.

After a while a whole range of metaphors will emerge from the data bank of words. This is where it is getting interesting because all metaphors can now be grouped into various *categories*.

☞ **For example two Bemba-metaphors of motion:**

Umutima wapilibuka: the SEIC is turning round

This means: At this moment the *SEIC* is turning round; one has reached a point of wanting to give up on a certain thing or task.

> *Umutima nauwa: the SEIC has fallen down, is lying down flat on the ground*
>
> This means: To be in a situation where one is not able to think straight. All thinking is going round in circles. The *SEIC* is captivated by the same kind of thoughts, one is feeling depressed.

2.2   The Seat of the Intellect

2.2.1   Ask which *place/spot* or *organ* of the *body* is thought to be responsible for *intellectual activities* like thinking, wanting, remembering, contemplating, planning etc.

> a.   It is very important to collect whole sentences and phrases!
>
> Again one might make use of three leading questions:
>
> 1.   What is the respective intellectual activity called?
>
> Result: One gets a certain word.
>
> 2.   What else does this word mean?
>
> Result: One gets (ideally) all situations in which this intellectual activity plays a role.
>
> 3.   What kind of intellectual activity is meant?
>
> Result: One gets the term that heads a certain domain of terms.
>
> b.   The data gathered will most probably ascertain that the location or organ of the body which was identified as the place where intellectual processes take place is *identical* with the seat of emotions!

☞   **Important:**

> As a lead: In English or in German one can say "I thought in my heart" (Ich dachte in meinem Herzen) or "He planned evil in his heart" (Er plante oder überlegte Böses in seinem Herzen).
>
> c.   That means: *feeling and thinking* are in terms of language and perception both understood as sharing one and the same source. This kind of arrangement is quite different from the euroamerican setup where each activity is assigned its own location.
>
> d.   Many languages lack extensive vocabulary with regard to the *head* as the prime faculty of intellectual processes. One might probe this issue further and come up with a set of questions.

☞   **Important:**

> Collect as many sentences as possible in which the "head" is thought to be the source of intellectual processes.

Include following words in the questionnaire: *intentions, abilities, knowledge, gifts or talents, memories, reflection, thoughts etc.*

2.3   The Seat of Character Attributes

2.3.1   Collect as many words and phrases which designate *character attributes* or *permanent psychic dispositions.*

❑ **Important:**

The word for character is a term that designates permanent features about a person.

The islanders of Chuuk call the permanent psychic dispositions of a person *tiip.*

Additional reading: **Käser** 1977: 49ff.

The Bemba of Zambia call permanent psychic dispositions *imibele,* derived from the word *ukubeela* which is the applied form of the intransitive verb *ukuba.* The meaning of *ukuba* is "being". However, its primary meaning is *"becoming".*

One is what he has become. *Imibele* are the result of a process that went on over time.

Additional reading: **Badenberg** 1999/2002, Chap. 4.

   a. Design a spread sheet with permanent psychic dispositions in your own language.

   b. Separate them into good (positive) and bad (negative) dispositions.

Ask your informant for the indigenous words describing permanent psychic dispositions.

Again one might make use of three leading questions:

   1. What is the respective character attribute called?

     Result: One gets a certain word.

   2. What else does this word mean?

     Result: One gets (ideally) all situations in which this character attribute plays a role or to which this character attribute is assigned.

   3. What kind of character attribute is meant?

     Result: One gets a term that heads a certain domain of terms.

Take the spread sheets with the vocabulary of permanent psychic dispositions in your own language and ask for the equivalent words or phrases in the informant's language.

If you give a negative character attribute, ask your informants whether they would also designate it as a negative character attribute! Do the same with each positive character-attribute.

Design data banks of words for *positive* and *negative* character attributes in the vernacular.

Look out for *idioms*, *proverbs* and *songs* which speak of the the personality of a person.

❑ **Important:**

> As the data banks on permanent psychic dispositions expand, one can begin to sort them – next to good or bad attributes – also into their metaphorical features. These metaphors can then be divided up into various *categories.*

⇨ **For example two Bemba-metaphors of *motion*:**

Umutima wa kupilibuka: a SEIC that "turns"

Permanent psychic disposition: one who constantly "turns" from one thing to another [changes opinions, changes places of work, is unstable in all he does and thinks].

Umutima uuwa: a SEIC that "falls down"

Permanent psychic disposition: one who always "falls down" [never be serious about something, always talking nonsense, lacking seriousness in all undertakings]; one whose *SEIC* has lost stability, has lost its moorings.

⇨ **For example two Chuuk-metaphors of *motion*:**

kun: the SEIC is turning

A person's interest is focused on certain things or matters caused by a turning of the *SEIC*. If one fails to grasp a certain matter or understand a certain issue, reasons for failure might be sought in a person's *SEIC* that does not point in the right direction. Also, it is possible to block a person's understanding by turning/twisting his/her *SEIC* (*okunnu neetipan*). This expression can be used in similar manner to describe the action of leading a person on the right path or leading him/her to go astray.

ttur: the SEIC "is falling down", "has fallen down"

This word expresses all feelings of disappointment, listlessness, despondency, hopelessness; but not the lack of courage or of feelings of fear (in Käser, 1977:62).

2.3.2   It is now important to find out if this body location on the body or this organ, which is identified to be associated with the emotions and the in-

tellectual processes, is also identified as the location or organ which is associated with *permanent psychic dispositions* or *personality traits*.

It can be seen from the Bemba examples that *umutima* (heart/*SEIC*) is the organ where *feelings* and *emotions* are registered, where *mental processes* occur, and at the same time where permanent *psychic dispositions* or *personality traits* reside.

It follows that the *SEIC* covers the <u>intellect</u> and all dispositions, both temporary (emotions) and permanent (character) that are present in a person!

❑ **Important:**

It should now be finally clear why it is more than just difficult to involve the English term 'soul' in the research. Although it covers things to do with the soul, i.e. feelings and emotions, it is *impossible* to link it with a person's permanent psychic dispositions.

One should be able to assume that the data bank that has emerged from the questions put to the informants proves unambiguously that the *seat of the emotions*, *intellect* and *character* is identified with one and the same organ or one and the same location on the body!

For this reason it is appropriate to replace the term psyche with the acronym SEIC, because it completely covers the seat of the feelings and emotions, the permanent psychic dispositions or personality traits, and the intellect!

These facts are in stark contrast to European-Western notions, for the latter reveal a strict conceptual divide between 'head' and 'heart'.

To underscore what was said earlier on, many ethnic groups do differentiate between feelings which can occur on *all* body parts and feelings which manifest themselves at only *one* location or in *one* organ. This location or organ is the *seat of emotions*.

This location or organ is usually also the location or the organ which is associated with the *intellect* and the *character* of a human being.

For this reason it is appropriate and logical when speaking of a human being to speak of his material body and his SEIC!

2.3.3 At this point a brief insert seems to be appropriate in order to draw attention to an important issue. Since *E*motions, the *I*ntellect and *C*haracter attributes are packaged together and are associated with a certain location or a certain organ, it follows that this spot or organ is the centre where ethical and moral norms that guide human action are situated. **In other words, the term that designates the *SEIC* is simultaneously the term that designates the *conscience*.**

Additional reading: **Käser** *Animism*, Chap. 10.

The following questions may be of help for further exploration.

2.3.4 Where does one have feelings of uneasiness when someone knows that he/she has committed a wrong or has breached a cultural norm?

a. What location or what organ is associated with breaching or breaking cultural norms or committing a wrong?

☞ **Important:**

These questions serve to ascertain that:

- the "conscience" is associated with a certain location or a certain organ.

- that this location or this organ is identical with the *SEIC*.

⇨ **Example:**

In Hebrew thinking emotions are associated with the heart (*leb*), but the most subtle feelings of a person are linked to the kidneys (*kabed*).

☞ **Hint:**

Conscience—as a term—is mostly discussed in the field of morality and within theological literature. Ethnological and psychological literature use terms like 'super-ego', or 'ego-ideal'.

Guilt-oriented cultures tend to socialize its members in such a way that they develop a ***super-ego***. That is, people who grow up within guilt-oriented social structures internalize not only the rules and norms of their social group and the wider culture, but also the persons who embody and personify them.

In contrast, shame-oriented cultures tend to socialize its members in such a way that they develop an ***ego-ideal***. That is, people are generally less worried about breaking a cultural norm. They are more worried about whether they can meet certain cultural norms or whether they will fall short of in meeting them.

Dominant factors are not the fear of breaking norms or the fear of sanctions when norms have been broken, but the fear of suffering the withdrawal of the social group, losing the right to be a fully accepted member of the group or even having to suffer the fate of an outcast. Emotions of denial and the feelings of being forsaken, that one would have to deal with, are powerful motivational forces that make people follow cultural norms and rules.

Additional reading: **Lomen** 2003, Chap. 2 and **Wiher** 2003, Chap. 2.

b. Advice: make a list or open a database with words and phrases that cover the topic conscience in your own mother-tongue.

c. It is advisable to collect as many phrases and examples as possible which express the idea that a person's conscience has been "activated".

d. Ask for the feelings (note the words) a person has when he/she *follows cultural norms*, that is, has a good conscience. Note: conformity to cultural norms refers always to the norms and values of the informant's culture.

e. Ask, where these feelings are manifest—which body location, which body organ?

f. Ask for the feelings (note the words) a person has when he/she does *not follow cultural norms*, that is, has a bad conscience. Note: nonconformity to cultural norms refers always to the norms and values of the informant's culture.

2.3.5 Do all living beings possess a *SEIC*?

a. What kinds of living beings do possess a *SEIC*?

b. Do all human beings possess a *SEIC*?

c. What kinds of persons are thought to possess a special kind of *SEIC*?

d. How, under what circumstances, can those persons come to possess such a special kind of *SEIC*?

e. Do handicapped people possess a *SEIC*?

f. In what way is their *SEIC* different from that of other persons?

g. Do mentally retarded persons possess a *SEIC?*

h. If so, what is the capacity of such a *SEIC*?

i. Do animals possess a *SEIC*?

j. Do all animals posses a *SEIC*?

k. Do certain animals ("sacred animals", "clan or totem-animals") possess a special kind of *SEIC*?

l. In what way is the *SEIC* of a person different from the *SEIC* of an animal?

m. Are there means "to tap into" the *SEIC* of an animal, a special animal?

n. Can the *SEIC* of a person be exchanged with the *SEIC* of an animal?

o. If so, what are the conditions? Under which circumstances?

p. Is such an exchange of *SEICs* temporary – for instance, for one night – or can one effect an exchange of *SEICs* over a longer period of time. Even permanently?

q. What happens when a person takes on the *SEIC* of an animal?

2.4   The Formation of the *SEIC*

2.4.1   Is a person born with a *SEIC* (use the indigenous term)?

a. If so, how is the *SEIC* described in linguistic terms?

b. Ask the informant/s to describe the *SEIC* as comprehensively as possible. Look out for adjectives: the *SEIC* is *soft, empty, little, small, formless, closed, transparent, hidden* etc.

2.4.2   If not, at what time after birth does a human being receive his/her *SEIC*?

❑ **Important:**

It is very possible that up to the time when the *SEIC* is acquired, a newborn baby is *not* regarded as a human being. Proof of this phenomenon could be linguistic evidence, that is, a specific term that designates newborn babies.

⇨ **Example:**

In Bemba, a newborn baby is called *Katuutu.* Etymologically, the following observations can be made:

Ka is prepositional and is of the diminutive class of words which expresses smallness or fineness with regard to size, shape (form, design) or quantity.

-tuutu is adjectival and carries the idea of whiteness (connoting purity) or transparency (connoting emptiness).

Katuutu – a tiny, little transparent (empty) 'thing'.

2.4.3   Does the moment at which the remainder of the severed umbilical cord is finally falling off mark an event that is of special importance to the *SEIC* of the child? That is to say: Does this event make a child to become a full human being?

a. When will the umbilical cord be severed from the body of the child?

b. Who severs and removes the umbilical cord?

    c. What happens to the umbilical cord?

    d. Where and how is the umbilical cord disposed of?

    e. Who is taking care of this?

2.4.4 Is there a special ceremony in which the child receives its name?

    a. All cultures attach great significance to the name or names of a person. Everywhere people bear names and their humanness is tied to a name.

    b. Do people believe that in giving a name – and more specifically the name of a dead ancestor – the *SEIC* of a person gets "activated"?

    c. What is done or what measures are taken so that a person acquires a *SEIC* after birth?

  ☞ **Important:**

      Collect linguistic material on the issue of name-giving and record name-giving rituals and ceremonies.

2.4.5 In what way can the *SEIC* of a person be caused 'to grow' or 'to develop'?

    a. Do the parents, grandparents or other relatives have a specific task in promoting or encouraging the 'development' or the 'growth' of the *SEIC* of a child?

    b. If yes, what do parents, grandparents or relatives do to promote or encourage the process of 'developing' or making the *SEIC* 'to grow'?

2.4.6 Use *participant observation* to gain a better understanding on how parents educate their children up to the age of 6 to 8 years: e.g. forceful and frequent admonition or reprimands, soft speech, frequent or rare corporal punishment, scaremongering or shaming them etc.)

    a. Is there linguistic evidence about the involvement of a spirit being in the 'development' or the 'growth' of the *SEIC* of a child?

    b. Do people talk frequently and quite 'naturally' about a spirit being's involvement in the 'development' or 'growth' of a child's *SEIC*?

In the section on *the seat of the character* an example from the Bemba language was used to show that from a linguistic perspective a person's character (the personality traits/*Imibele*) is the result of a *process*.

A person *is*, what he or she **has become**! That is, among the Bemba a person's *SEIC* is subjected to a 'becoming' which can be either promoted or impeded.

c. Does the ethnic group have similar notions in connection with the sphere of work?

d. How is this process of the emergence of personality traits realised?

☞ **Important:**

> At this point there is an issue that needs to be briefly anticipated. It has been shown form the language that among the Bemba the spirit being *umupashi*, which accompanies each person during his or her lifetime, exercises a causal effect on that person. (There will be more on the linguistic analysis of the term *umupashi* in the next chapter).

> In other words, *umupashi* is significantly involved in the formation of a person's *SEIC*. The causal effect of *umupashi* on a person is connected with the giving of the name. *Katuutu* becomes a person through the name.

> Now *umupashi* starts the character formation, or in other words the shaping of the personality traits *(Imibele)* in the child's *SEIC*, which in the **process** of growing up become more and more apparent from the outside, or getting bigger or more mature.

> In discussing *the seat of the character* it has already been pointed out that *Imibele* is derived from the intransitive verb *ukuba* = **to be, but more precisely** *to become*. A person's *Imibele* describe his 'becoming', or what he **has become**.

> *Imibele* can be a feature not only of persons, plants and animals but also of objects. In addition they can be divided into *Imibele iisuma* (good, beautiful, positive *imibele*) and *Imibele iibi* (bad, negative *imibele*). *Imibele* are permanently present psychic dispositions.

> Among the Bemba of Zambia the process of the growth of a person's *SEIC* can be illustrated in the language from three examples:

(1) *Ukumoneka ne mibele* = to appear with *Imibele*, step into the outside, into the light, become visible with them. A child *appears* **with Imibele,** *steps outside* **with Imibele.**

(2) *Ukukula ne mibele* = grow, become big or mature with *imibele*. A child *grows, becomes bigger, "matures"* **with Imibele.** In both examples plays the conjunction *ne (with)* a decisive part.

> The linguistic analysis reflects the notion that a child does not **have** personality traits, but that, while not being innately possessed by him, they emerge in him and become larger and

more mature. This means that what 'becomes' or 'has become' through the process of influence on the child's *SEIC* exercised by the spirit being *umupashi,* by its *SEIC,* becomes visible.

(3) *Ukulango mibele* = to show *Imibele,* that is, make the hidden visible. This means that previously invisible or unnoticeable personality traits *(Imibele)* can now be perceived or indicated by others.

Additional reading: **Badenberg** 1999/2002, Chap. 4.

e. What *actions*, what *behaviour* on the part of the family and the social group among which the child grows up, *help* the spirit being to do its 'work' without disruption?

f. What *actions*, what *behaviour* on the part of the family and the social group among which the child grows up, *prevent* or *hinder* the spirit being from doing its 'work' properly?

2.5   Influencing the *SEIC* through Spirit Beings

2.5.1 At what times does or can a spirit being exert influence on a person's *SEIC*?

a. When it is near that person?

b. When it is in direct body contact with that person?

2.5.2 How does the presence or the body contact of a spirit being influence a person's *SEIC*?

a. Does that person experience a positive emotional mood?

b. Does that person exhibit greater intellectual powers?

c. Is there evidence that the influence a *benevolent* spirit being can exert on the *SEIC* of a person produces behaviour that conforms to cultural norms?

d. In what way does closeness or body contact of a *malevolent* spirit being influence the *SEIC* of a person?

e. What kind of emotional moods, through the influence of malevolent spirit beings, can be noticed or observed in the *SEIC* of a person?

f. In what measure, in what ways are aggressiveness, raving madness, yelling or non-conformity with regard to cultural laws ascribed to the influence of a malevolent spirit being on the *SEIC* of a person?

g. What kinds of emotions are most prominent in people who experience the influence of a malevolent spirit being on their *SEIC*?

h. Is the behaviour of a person who shows the emotions which are thought to be caused by the activity of a malevolent spirit being excusable? Do others hold them accountable for their behaviour although a malevolent spirit being is thought to be the cause?

i. Does the influence or activity of a malevolent spirit being on the *SEIC* of a person reduce his or her intellectual capability or productivity?

2.6 Influencing the *SEIC* through Medicine

2.6.1 If through closeness or even body contact of a malevolent spirit being the *SEIC* of a person has become affected, can he/she be helped by medicine or certain medication?

a. How is this particular type of medicine called? Is there a generic term for this type of medicine?

b. Does the generic term of this type of medicine already hint at a class of medicine, a special category of medicine?

⇨ **Example:**

The islanders of Chuuk call this medicine *sáfeen asaram* which can be translated as "medicine of illumination" (Käser 2014:151).

c. On what attributes is the healing power of the medicine for the *SEIC* of a person based?

- What role do the *visible* attributes of substances play?

- What role do the *tangible* attributes of substances play?

- What role do the attributes of substances that can be *smelled* play?

2.6.2 Which analogies between the attributes, the form or the colour of a certain medicine and the effects it is expected to have on people are of importance?

⇨ **Example:**

Among the Bemba of Zambia there are a lot of categories which are classified in terms of medicine. For example, if a wife has concerns about her husband's faithfulness she can induce a change of disposition, i.e. a change in her husband's *SEIC*, through an appropriate medicine from the category *umuti wa cisense* or *umuti wa kutemwikwa* ("medicine for being loved or liked" (This category includes [all] drugs which come under socalled *love magic*).

One drug which is secretly administered to a husband contains parts of a gecko – the omnipresent little lizard often found residing in the house, and in great numbers. Such a medicine imparts to the husband the attribute of the gecko – a domestic tendency. Success is shown in a noticeable "domesticity" of the husband.

Such a situation, indicating that the husband is dutiful and domesticated, can be described as *ukupilibulo mutima* = the *SEIC* has been completely turned round.

Naturally a similar procedure is available if a person is suspected of suffering from negative emotional moods or a severe decline in intellectual capability through the influence of a malevolent spirit being.

In such cases, it is also expected that medicine or medication which is produced according to the logic of analogy produces the desired effects and results.

  a. Is there a kind of medicine that can and does exert influence on the-*SEIC* of a (benevolent) spirit being?

  b. Can (or must) this medicine be part of an offering?

2.6.3 What occasions require a shaman, a healer or a medium to have a particularly alert *SEIC* and, with the assistance of special medicine, to solve a difficult task?

☞ **Hint:**

Pay attention to the adjectives with which an alert SEIC is associated with (e.g. medicine which "***enlightens***" or "***illuminates***" the SEIC of a person).

  a. What are situations in which ordinary persons make use of medicine that can further the capacities of their *SEIC* or that will give ***enhanced performances*** to their *SEIC*?

  b. What is this medicine called?

  c. What are the substances of plants that provide the ingredients for this medicine (take note of their names)?

  d. Likewise, is there medicine that can ***"weaken"*** a person's *SEIC*?

  e. What is this medicine called?

  f. What are the substances of plants that provide the ingredients for this medicine (take note of their names and habitats)?

  g. Who can produce this medicine?

  h. On what occasions is medicine that "weakens" or "dims" a person's *SEIC* produced and administered?

☞ **Hint:**

Take note of the adjectives describing the medicine that "weakens" or "dims" a person's *SEIC*.

i.   What medicine "weakens" or "dims" a person's *SEIC*?

j.   How is the idea of "weakening" or "dimming" a person's *SEIC* expressed in the language concerned?

k.   Are there other adjectives that express the same idea?

2.7   Influencing the *SEIC* through Learning and Understanding

2.7.1   As well as the external influences spirit beings or certain traditional medicine can have on the *SEIC* of people, one other dimension is also of importance.

This dimension includes all ideas about learning, comprehending, having profound knowledge in a specific field of human life or the world in which we live. To bring to light how this dimension of learning, comprehension and knowledge is structured, linguistic research might provide interesting and important insights.

First, one may begin by collecting all words and phrases which speak of learning, understanding, to practise something, to rehearse etc.

a.   What is the word for learning, studying?

b.   How does one say: "to have learned something", "to have acquired understanding", "to have studied a matter" etc.?

c.   How does one say: "to practise a song", "to rehearse a dance" etc.?

d.   What is the word for understanding ("I understand", "I got it" or "to have an understanding of a certain matter", "to have full comprehension of something")?

e.   How does one say: "to have understood a thing", "to have grasped a certain matter", or "I see what you mean"?

2.7.2   By collecting as many phrases and contexts as possible, one can discover the metaphorical expressions with which people make reference to when someone has learned a particular thing, when one has understood or comprehended a certain matter.

⇨ **Example:**

In English one can say: "to imbibe something", meaning: "to have got a thing into one's head", that is, to have internalised a thing, to have firmly grasped a thing.

The Bemba language establishes a close connection between "listening" and "understanding", "comprehending". The verb *ukumfwa* expresses both activities. Only a person who really listens (*umfweni* = listen!) is able to understand, comprehend (*waumfwa?* = have you understood, have you got it?). Also: a person who has understood or comprehended a thing (*naumfwa* = I have understood) is one who really listens: (*ulya alomfwa* = that one listens).

2.8   The Development of the *SEIC*

It was already been pointed out that the *SEIC* of a child may be metaphorically described as ***soft, empty, small, formless or closed.*** As a person grows older, the metaphors for the *SEIC* of a person change and are substituted with other metaphors.

a.   Which metaphorical expressions are in use within particular age groups (adolescents, married people, bearers of status, the elderly etc.?

☞ **Hint:**

Adjectives like "big/ large", "hard" or "open" may provide important hints on the development of the *SEIC* of a person. Maybe other adjectives like "voluminous", "enlarged" or "expanded" or "mature" are of importance too.

b.   Does the 'enlargement' or the 'expansion' of the *SEIC* cause a person to be able to increasingly differentiate emotions?

c.   Does the 'hardening' of the *SEIC* describe the formation of the will power or the character of a person?

d.   Does the 'openness' of the *SEIC* indicate to what extend or to what degree a person's intellectual power has been unfolded, has been expanded?

e.   Does the *SEIC* of a person undergo a process of change, that is, with increasing age the *SEIC* is first 'growing', 'expanding', then it will be 'harder', then be 'wider' and finally reach a state of maturity (complete 'openness')?

f.   Which personality traits are thought to match an 'enlarged', 'hardened' or 'opened' *SEIC* of a person?

g.   What are the outstanding personality traits (e.g. high level of enduring frustration) which indicate an extraordinary high 'openness', an extraordinary 'enlarged' or 'hardened' *SEIC*?

h.   When a person maintains an 'opened', 'enlarged' or a 'non-hardened' *SEIC* into old age, what do people call such persons? Which words do they use to describe them?

i. Are such individuals seen or regarded as wise persons?

j. Do they enjoy special treatment or are they counted as persons of higher status?

k. What effects does the ageing of the body have on the *SEIC* of a person? Or in other words:

l. What influence do the changes of the *SEIC* during the various stages of life have on the ageing process of the body?

m. In what way is the acquisition of language, the ability to speak properly, understood as a direct outcome or result of the development of the *SEIC*?

n. Would a child learn its mother-tongue if nobody talked to it in that language?

o. If yes, how do people think the process of learning the language could happen?

p. How would a child learn all the words and the proper use of them?

Chapter 3
The Being that Survives the Death of the Body

> This chapter explains how one can structure research in order to cover another dimension of the concept of man of ethnic groups: *what* kind of spirit beings play a significant role in their cultural world; *what* words or phrases are in use that designate and describe the being that survives the death of the body; *how* the predominant spirit double of a person can be identified; *how* the name of a person might relate to his or her dream-ego; *what* kind of relationship might exist between the loss or absence of one's dream-ego and illnesses; *how* the dream-ego and the *SEIC* of a person relate to one another and *what* kind of linguistic relationship might exist between the dream-ego, the shadow of a person and the mirror image of a person.

3.0   Introduction

The death of the body is a dramatic and often very painful experience of human existence in all societies on earth. The effects of death are so profound because the death of the body means that **all** functions of the *SEIC* of a person have come to a final halt. Everything that has characterised the *SEIC* as the seat of emotions, of the intellectual processes, and the personality traits/character attributes are gone; all personality traits of a person's corporeal *SEIC* are temporary. That means, *the SEIC of a person is part of being human while alive, but lacks capacity to exist beyond the death of the body.*

The concept of man in many traditional societies often contains, however, very detailed ideas and concepts about the existence of a person after the death of the body. One concept that can be found across the board in traditional societies is the idea that next to the temporal, corporeal *SEIC* of a Person there *exists* also *another SEIC* which continues on and preserves the personality traits of a person even after the death of the body.

It is of importance to stress at this point that one should abstain from using the word "soul" at all. One should always make use of the indigenous words and phrases and only be concerned with their linguistic and social load. How these words and phrases as well as their particular content and meaning can be researched will be the subject of this chapter.

As a rule of thumb: Always look out for the word or phrase that designates the *being that survives the death of the body and perpetuates the personality of a person!* Only then can meaningful statements about the existence of a person after the death of his/her body be made.

3.1 The Designation of the Being that Survives the Death of the Body

3.1.1 What is the word for the being that survives the death of the body?

❑ **Important:**

Avoid using the word "part" (e.g. "what part of a person survives after death" etc.). One should always bear in mind that in non-western societies, man does not exist as a sum of parts.

Ask questions like:

a. What happens to a person when he or she is dying?

b. When a person dies, what is the name of the being that separates from and survives the death of the body?

c. When a corpse is buried, cremated or simply left to decay, in what form or as what kind of a being does the person continue to exist?

d. Does this being continue the personality of the dead person?

☞ **Hint:**

In some societies it is taboo to speak about deceased persons or to even mention their names. Keep the question in a general context. The Yanomami of Venezuela, for example, are very particular about deceased members of their groups.

See: **Ritchie** 2000. *Spirit of the Rainforest.*

e. Is the word that was asked for a ***noun***?

f. Is the word stem a ***verb***?

☞ **Hint:**

If yes, it would mean that the being which lives on after the death of the body is sometimes associated with an activity or even exercises a causative influence on living persons! The verb stem could express something like the 'chief quality' of the spirit being.

⇨ **Example:**

The Bemba word for the being that lives on after the death of the body is *umupashi.*

The word *umupashi* is a noun and belongs grammatically to the group of nouns which includes many of the body parts and organs, especially the most important ones.

[Bemba is a Bantu language with the feature that all nouns are divided into classes].

In my opinion the root of *umupashi* is derived from the transitive, causative verb *ukupasha* (to bring about a similarity, resemble something, inherit traits, features and qualities – both good and bad).

This leads to the following definition for the being summed up in the language as *umupashi*:

a) *Umupashi* is a spirit being strongly associated with the body (*umubili*) of a person (*umuntu*) (this is indicated by the first syllable *umu-*). This syllable is the marker of the noun class referring to being human. It includes also many parts and organs of the body.

b) But there is another aspect which is of great significance: *umupashi* is associated with the person in another way apart from the body. This association is very clearly apparent in the metaphor of the language and is rooted in the transitive verb *ukupasha* (to **bring about a similarity, resemble something, inherit traits, features and qualities – both good and bad**).

Additional reading: **Badenberg** 2003:322-324.

Consequently *umupashi* has a causative effect on a person. In other words, *umupashi* passes on certain **traits, personality features** or **qualities** to the person assigned to it, so that this person can become a real human being!

g. It is absolutely critical to collect as many phrases and idioms as possible in which the word is used. Data can then be analysed:

- of importance are all the various contexts in which this word is used.

- also, all **derivations** of this word are important and should be further analysed!

☞ **Important:**

It is very possible to find that human beings are associated with more than just one spirit being which accompany a person all his/her life and also survive the death of his/her body. Sometimes a person has two, three or even dozens of accompanying spirit beings!

Additional reading: **Käser** *Animism*, Chap. 11.

This fact extremely complicates the research at times because all of them require further investigation and their own question-naires. More on the topic of other spirit beings is found in the following section.

3.2 Other Spirit Beings

3.2.1 What are these other spirit beings called?

☞ **Hint:**

The indigenous words and terms are important! Collect words and terms and put them into a database/spreadsheet.

3.2.2 What is it that these other spirit beings have in common? Do they share common *linguistic* features?

3.2.3 If not, do they share similar *functions*?

3.2.4 If not, do they share common *features* in their appearance (some sort of body or form resemblance) or in the way they are associated with human beings?

☞ **Hint:**

One has to bear in mind that not all of the afore-mentioned aspects are applicable to all of these other spirit beings to the same extent. More data needs to be collected. The following questions may serve as a guide:

3.2.5 Are these other spirit beings thought to inhabit the same "heavenly realms/spheres"?

☞ **Hint:**

Search for the words for sky, heaven, heavens, heavenly abode etc. Which of the terms are associated with the habitat of these other spirit beings?

3.2.6 Have all of these other spirit beings the ability to extricate themselves from the effects of space and time, that is, distance and matter do not pose any problem to them?

3.2.7 Have all of these other spirit beings the ability to penetrate the human body/take possession of the body?

3.2.8 Does possession cause organic and/or personality disorders?

3.2.9 **A distinct feature of spirit beings is that they are without a body, a material body. Their spirit nature can however allow for manifestation in certain *forms*.**

⇨ **Example:**

Among the Bemba in Zambia one can find the belief that a whirlwind signals the presence of a spirit being or spirit beings.

Therefore, one should look out for kinds of visible manifestation which people believe signal the presence of spirit beings.

3.2.10 **Are spirit beings religious? Do they adhere to a certain religion?**

☞ **Hint:**

Within Islamic societies the idea exists that spirit beings subscribe to *religion*. It is therefore quite logical for Islamic societies to perceive them as Muslims.

3.2.11 **Once the majority of terms for spirit beings have been collected and analysed, the nature of spirit beings can now be further investigated.**

☞ **Hint:**

The *attributes* and *characteristics* of those spirit beings are essential and really important.

3.3   Malevolent Spirit Beings

☞ **Hint:**

Malevolent, evil spirits are in general on hostile terms with people and seek to cause them harm. (Käser 2014:91).

As well as the adjective 'malevolent' or 'evil' there may even be other adjectives of importance like: 'aggressive,' 'hostile', 'bad' or 'mean'.

It is advisable to design a separate data bank for this kind of malevolent spirit beings.

3.3.1 **Which of these spirit beings can be associated with the adjective *evil*, *aggressive, hostile, bad, mean* etc.?**

3.3.2 ***Evil* spirits, that is, those who can be judged on the grounds of their bad psychic-moral attributes can be further examined by determining their *corporeal attributes* or *characteristics*.**

     a. Of what nature is their appearance, that is, do evil spirits appear in animal form (theriomorph) or in human form (anthropomorph)?

b. What is their *sexual behavior* like (wild, unbridled, excessive etc.)?

☞ **Hint:**

One needs to exercise care and sensitiveness here. Ask informants of the same sex.

c. What kind of *external characteristics* do they possess (grimace, features of a monster, abnormal limbs, caricature of animals etc.)?

d. Are they considered to be *cold* beings, that is, is their body temperature lower than that of other living beings?

e. What can be said of their *body odour* (disgusting, repulsive, aversive, nauseating, sickening, loathsome)?

☞ **Hint:**

Establish categories of features or attributes as outlined above and sort or group malevolent spirit beings accordingly.

f. How about their skills in terms of articulation and language usage?

g. Are they able to speak well and articulate?

h. Are they able to speak clearly and articulately in a foreign language?

i. What kind of foreign languages can they speak? How many do they master?

j. Do they possess exceptionally good sight?

k. Do they possess hearing?

l. Do they possess abilities to hear extraordinary well?

m. Do they need food?

n. Do they have "favourite dishes"?

o. Can they or do they have to eat regularly?

p. How about their sense of taste?

q. What kind of food or dishes are not to the liking of their sense of taste at all.

r. What food is appalling to them?

s. How about their sense of smell?

t. What kinds of smells will keep them at bay or will keep them at a distance?

☞ **Hint:**

People in Pasundan (Indonesia) are of the opinion that the awful smell of smoke of certain cigars will drive away evil spirits (Knödler 2006).

u. What kinds of customs and rituals are in place in order to keep evil spirits at a distance through certain smells and food items?

v. Are **water spirits,** in comparison with other evil spirits, particularly prone to aggressiveness and violent behaviour?

w. If yes, how does their marked aggressiveness show?

x. Which locations or places are in particular associated with evil spirits?

☞ **Hint:**

Some ethnic groups consider the sewer system or toilets to be the dwelling place of malevolent spirit beings. Such localities can therefore pose a definite threat to humans.

y. What traces or marks can or do malevolent spirit beings leave on humans or material things (e.g. bruises, scratches, footprints etc.)?

3.3.3 *Malevolent* **spirit beings can be described in even more detail as one researches their** *psychic-intellectual capabilities* **or** *attributes.*

a. Do malevolent spirit beings have *emotions*?

☞ **Hint:**

Work with spread sheets and record the words for emotions that apply to malevolent spirit beings.

b. What location or organ can be identified as the seat of emotions?

c. Is *fear* an emotion that can be ascribed to them?

d. What, who or which kind of objects can trigger an emotion of fear or anxiety in them?

☞ **Hint:**

Certain stones, metal or salt could be of great importance.

e. Can malevolent spirit beings suffer a state of anxiety?

f. What role do amulets or objects of everyday life play?

g. How to malevolent spirits react to *colours*?

h. Which colours do they fear most?

i. What role does the colour red play? Do they have a particular fear of red?

j. What *intellectual capacity* do malevolent spirit beings possess?

> ☞ **Hint:**
>
> A database/spreadsheet of terms which are applicable to them might prove very valuable and the collected language material could lead to astonishing results.

k. Where do their intellectual processes take place?

l. What locations on the body or which body organ is predominantly associated with intellectual processes?

m. Which adjectives describe the intellectual capacity of malevolent spirit beings (e.g. "dull", "stupid", "simple" etc.)?

n. What measures can a person take in order to deceive, mislead, out-wit or fool a malevolent spirit being?

o. What happens or what may happen when a malevolent spirit being sees its own image in a mirror?

p. Are there traditions or practices which make use of a mirror in order to put malevolent spirit beings to flight when they see their image in the mirror?

> ☞ **Hint:**
>
> Some ethnic groups hang small mirror pieces on their outer garments or affix them on their clothes (especially so on the clothing of children). Malevolent spirit beings are meant to be frightened and put to flight when catching sight of their own image in the mirror pieces.

3.3.4 What kind of *character attributes* can be ascribed to malevolent spirit beings?

☞ **Hint:**

One may simply use the database/spreadsheet that contains the language material with regard to permanent psychic dispositions of humans.

a. Where are permanent psychic dispositions localised in malevolent spirit beings?

b. Which locations on the body or which body organs are thought to represent the place where permanent psychic dispositions are localised?

   c. Which adjectives describe permanent psychic dispositions of malevolent spirit beings?

   d. In what ways do permanent psychic dispositions of malevolent spirit beings show considerable deficiencies?

   e. To what extent are malevolent spirit beings, due to their permanent psychic dispositions (character traits), put on the same level as animals?

☞ **Important:**

> The reason why such detailed information on these spirit beings is to be gathered is to find out whether they possess a *SEIC* of their own. Because then it could be ascertained that they are beings with their own identity, their own personality.
>
> Malevolent spirits can also be classified as ***malevolent spirit doubles!***
>
> Everything that is true with regard to ***corporeal attributes*** and ***psychic-intellectual capabilities*** is also true of ***benevolent spirit beings***. More on this topic in the section: 'benevolent spirit beings.'

3.3.5 What kind of *illnesses* can malevolent spirit beings cause in human beings?

☞ **Hint:**

> As a starting point one could begin to research the more obvious causes of illnesses and then concentrate on the causes which are not so obvious. Illnesses not obviously caused by malevolent spirit beings include many kinds of infections, paralytic ailments, gynaecological complaints, impotence in men etc.

   a. In what ways can malevolent spirit beings cause such sicknesses in people?

     ☞ **Hint:**

> A widespread behaviour of malevolent spirit beings is their habit of ***biting.*** Their ability to bite is not restricted to external attacks. Malevolent spirit beings may place bites externally as well as internally. Worth noting is definitely how people, linguistically express such 'biting' of malevolent spirit beings.
>
> • What kind of vocabulary is used to describe such incidences?
>
> • Which verbs are most prominent in connection with certain foods (e.g. 'eat', 'devour', 'swallow', etc.)?

Additional reading: **Käser** *Animism*, Chap. 8.

b. In what way are malevolent spirit beings, illness, treatment and the specialist involved linguistically related?

    ☞ **Hint:**

In some ethnic groups one can find that malevolent spirit beings xx may cause a certain illness xx, which gets treated by a certain ritual xx, and is carried out by a specialist xx. Noteworthy is the fact that xx is always the same word or phrase in the language concerned.

c. Have malevolent spirit beings the ability to enter the body of a person *unnoticed*?

d. What kind of precautionary measures would people take in order to protect themselves from unnoticed intrusions by malevolent spirit beings?

    ☞ **Hint:**

Some ethnic societies believe that an effective measure to prevent malevolent spirit beings from entering the body unnoticed is to place one's hand in front of the mouth while yawning.

e. Which are the favourite body locations for malevolent spirit beings to gain entrance to the interior of the body of a person?

f. What kinds of illnesses which are caused by malevolent spirit beings are treatable and moreover curable?

g. Who can treat and cure them?

h. Are there illnesses which are caused by malevolent spirit beings that are not treatable and moreover which are not curable?

3.3.6 What kinds of *"psychic states"* can malevolent spirit beings cause in human beings?

a. What effects does a 'bite' inflicted at the body location or on the organ which is recognized as the seat of emotions, the intellect, and the permanent psychic dispositions (*SEIC*) have?

b. To what extent are states of depression, listlessness, dragging oneself into doing something, a surly nature ascribed to the internal 'bite' by a malevolent spirit being?

c. In what ways are abnormal behaviours (e.g. rage, fury, irascibility, vandalism etc.) seen as results or effects of having been 'bitten' by a malevolent spirit being?

d. To what extent can speech impediments in people be traced back to the bite of a malevolent spirit being?

e. What are the possibilities of healing for people who are experiencing such psychic conditions due to the effect of a malevolent spirit being?

☞ **Hint:**

As a rule such psychic conditions are understood as *illness*. This can be ascertained by listening to how people talk about it, i.e. whether they refer to the affected person as 'ill'.

In this connection it might also be possible to ask how such psychic conditions – i.e. these kinds of illness – and possession are distinguished from each other as concepts.

One can assume that the activity of malevolent spirit beings (biting and the ensuing psychic conditions) are *not* regarded as phenomena connected with possession.

f. What kinds of medical treatment can help such a person?

g. Who has to prepare it?

h. What procedures have to accompany the production of this medicine?

i. From which plant substances (note the terms for them) are the active ingredients for this medicine acquired?

j. Can animals be "bitten" by malevolent spirit beings?

k. If yes, which animals are particularly endangered by the bite of a malevolent spirit being

l. To what extent are malevolent spirit beings also responsible for abnormal psychic dispositions in animals?

3.3.7 What kinds of influence may malevolent spirit beings exert on the conscience (super-ego or ego-ideal)?

a. In what sense are malevolent spirit beings understood to trigger bad thoughts?

b. In what sense are malevolent spirit beings understood to trigger destructive, evil actions in people?

3.3.8 In what measure are malevolent spirit beings responsible for *mental* or *physical handicaps* in people?

a. How do people refer to those in their own group who have unusual physical features (e.g. albinism, red hair)?

b. Which deformities in a person are attributed to the influence of a malevolent spirit being?

   c. When malevolent spirit beings intend to approach a woman, can they then change into men?

   d. Are deformed children then the result of such a sexual union?

     ☞ **Hint:**

     Find out if such a union and its result is blamed on the woman or whether she is regarded as a victim!

   e. What position in society is allocated to people with deformities?

   f. Are they permitted to live freely in the village community?

   g. Are there rules determining how to relate to such people?

   h. What are the differences in the education or upbringing of "normal" children and children with deformities?

   i. In what ways are children with deformities seen as bringing disgrace on the family?

   j. What attitudes of the family towards such children reveal this?

   k. What notions are apparent concerning particular foods which pregnant women should not eat, because the attributes of such foods could by analogy be transferred to the child?

     ☞ **Hint:**

     Among the Bemba (and related ethnic groups) in Zambia there is the notion that a pregnant woman should not eat eggs, or else the child will be born bald – as smooth as the top of an egg.

3.3.9 Where do malevolent spirits come from?

   a. Are there myths about the origin of malevolent spirits beings?

     ☞ **Hint:**

     Collect as many myths as possible.

   b. Do malevolent spirit beings have a beginning? Have they been created at one time in the past?

   c. Is their creator an especially powerful malevolent spirit?

   d. What is the name of this extraordinary powerful evil spirit being?

3.4 Benevolent Spirit Beings

☞ **Hint:**

Benevolent spirit beings are in general on friendly terms with people (Käser 2014:120).

As well as the adjective "good" may other adjectives like "peaceful" or "friendly" be of importance.

It is advisable to create a data bank that deals specifically with benevolent spirit beings.

3.4.1   What kind of spirit beings are described with the adjective *good*?

☞ **Hint:**

Collect all the names of these spirit beings. Design a spread sheet and record their names.

3.4.2   *Benevolent spirit beings* – whose main characteristics are their good psychic-moral attributes – do also show a number of *corporeal attributes*.

☞ **Hint:**

Benevolent spirit beings may bear rather human like features and could possibly be called something like: 'human spirits'.

A more accurate classification requires the collection by native speakers of as many as possible sentences which can then be linguistically analysed.

- a. Do benevolent spirit beings in general appear in human form (anthropomorph)?
- b. If so, is their appearance in human form identical to the external appearance of a person? Do they match completely in terms of outward appearance?
- c. Under what kind of circumstances do benevolent spirit beings appear in animal form (theriomorph)?
- d. How about height and weight of benevolent spirit beings? Anything that can be said about it?
- e. Can benevolent spirit beings fall sick? Do they ever fall sick?
- f. Do benevolent spirit beings suffer from handicaps or physical deformities?
- g. To what extent are benevolent spirit beings described with the adjectives "pretty", "beautiful", "handsome"?
- h. How do people speak of the "beauty" of benevolent spirit beings? What words/ phrases do they describe them with?
- i. Do benevolent spirit beings possess extraordinary physical strength?
- j. What kind of powerful and exceptional deeds are they accredited with because of their physical strength?

k. What kind of motions are they thought to be performing (dancing, walking, climbing, flying, swimming etc.)?

l. Do benevolent spirit beings have to breathe?

m. Do they have to sleep, that is, do they require sleep in order to re-generate and regain strength?

n. Do they always appear dressed up wearing ornaments and/or jewellery?

o. Does the kind of clothing and ornaments they wear correspond with the kinds of clothing and ornaments that are found among the ethnic group?

p. Are benevolent spirit beings regarded as 'warm' beings, that is, does their body temperature equal the body temperature of other living beings?

q. What can be said about their body odour?

r. Does their body odour draw human beings close to them, because their scent is so sweet, so attractive, so infatuating?

s. Are they able to laugh and to weep?

t. How about their speech abilities? Are they able to speak?

u. Are they able to speak clearly and articulately?

v. Are they fluent in foreign languages?

w. Can they sing in those languages?

> ☞ **Hint:**
>
> Some ethnic groups have a special kind of 'cult' language or a language that is used during the performance of rituals when contact with benevolent spirit beings is sought. Is that true of this ethnic group?

x. Which foreign languages can they speak?

y. How about their hearing?

z. Do they have special hearing abilities?

3.4.3 How about the *nourishment* of benevolent spirit beings?

a. Do they require nourishment, that is, do they have to eat?

b. What kinds of food or dishes are taboos for them?

c. What kinds of food or dishes are taboos for persons who are dealing with them in a special way or who have to rely on their help in a special way?

3.4.4 How about the *sense of smell* of benevolent spirit beings?

☞ **Hint:**

The fact that spirit beings possess a sense of smell is one of their outstanding and distinctive corporeal features or characteristics (Käser 2014:123).

a. Is their sense of smell exceptional or outstanding compared to the other senses?

b. How does an unpleasant smell affect benevolent spirit beings?

c. In what way does an unpleasant smell affect the emotions of benevolent spirit beings?

d. How do pleasant smells or fragrances affect benevolent spirit beings?

> ☞ **Hint:**
>
> People in Pasundan (Indonesia) believe that benevolent spirit beings regard the scent of continuous incense burning as pleasantly fragrant (Knödler 2006).

e. What kinds of smells are attractive or even seductive to benevolent spirit beings and would cause them to seek to be close to human beings?

f. What kinds of emotions in benevolent spirit beings are triggered by pleasant smells?

g. What kind of impression does bad human odour make on them?

h. What kinds of human odours can they stand the least?

i. Which purity laws are mandatory or obligatory for persons (mediums, shamans) who deal with benevolent spirit beings on a special basis?

j. What purity laws are especially applicable to women who engage in dealings with benevolent spirit beings?

k. What kinds of measures or precautions do menstruating women have to undertake?

l. Do menstruating women have to reckon with a lesser degree of protection from benevolent spirit beings during their time of "impurity"?

m. In what ways do menstruating women pose a danger to the members of their family or their social group?

n. Do menstruating women have to live in seclusion, that is, away from the community until their time is over?

o. Do menstruating women have to observe special rules/laws with regard to food?

p. Are there rules which prescribe menstruating women certain types of food?

q. Are there rules which prohibit menstruating women from partaking of certain types of food?

3.4.5 How is the sexual disposition of benevolent spirit beings to be graded?

☞ **Hint:**

It is advisable to be sensitive in dealing with this issue. Question informants of the same sex as yourself.

a. Are benevolent spirit beings in general *sexual beings*?

☞ **Hint:**

Here it is necessary to make a distinction. Are benevolent spirit beings sexual beings in the sense of being interested in sexual activity or are they sexual beings in the sense of their sexuality, i.e. male or female?

As far as the Bemba of Zambia are concerned the most important benevolent spirit beings are bisexual, and any interest in sexual activity recedes into the background.

The bisexuality of benevolent spirit beings appears to be mainly a Bantu phenomenon.

b. Are benevolent spirit beings involved in sexual relations?

c. Are sexual relations limited to their own kind or is their sexual interest also directed to people or animals?

d. Do benevolent spirit beings approach women in a base manner or is there such a thing as an official, formal union?

e. Do these unions produce so-called "spirit children"?

f. If yes, what is the indigenous term for such "spirit children"?

g. If yes, are such "spirit children" assigned to a person (a child) as a spirit double?

h. What kind of task is the responsibility of "spirit children" which are assigned to person as a spirit double?

i.   Are benevolent spirit beings limited by space and time?

j.   Do they prefer particular times of day for pursuing their activities?

k.   Are they able to make themselves visible at any time?

l.   Which persons have the possibility of perceiving benevolent spirit beings?

m.   What are the preconditions for people being able to perceive benevolent spirit beings (trance, dream, when awake)?

n.   What accompanying phenomena appear when they make themselves visible?

o.   What is the part played by light or luminescence?

p.   When they become visible, are benevolent spirit beings described in terms such as "figures of light"?

q.   What is the corresponding term for it?

3.4.6   *Benevolent spirit beings* **can in addition be described more precisely by asking about their *psychic and intellectual qualities.***

a.   Do benevolent spirit beings have ***emotions***?

b.   Which emotions are especially characteristic of them?

> ☞ **Hint:**
>
> It would be worth creating a databank of terms for the emotions that apply particularly here.

c.   Where is the ***seat*** of their emotions, i.e. which part of the body or which organ is identified with the seat of the emotions?

d.   Is ***fear*** one of the emotions that can be ascribed to them?

e.   Can they tolerate a "condition of fear"?

f.   Are they generally regarded as being friendly to people?

g.   How does this friendliness manifest itself?

h.   How to benevolent spirit beings react to colours?

i.   Which colour(s) do they particularly like?

j.   What ***intellectual capacities*** do benevolent spirit beings have?

> ☞ **Hint:**
>
> Here, too, a databank of applicable terms could produce astonishing results.

k. Where do their intellectual processes take place, i.e. which part of the body or organ is identified as the seat of the intellect?

l. What adjectives are used to describe the intelligence of benevolent spirit beings (e.g. 'clever', 'wise' etc.)?

m. What can a person do to encourage a benevolent spirit being to provide help?

n. What kinds of "supplications" can be made to them?

> ☞ **Hint:**
>
> A collection of such "supplications" could provide interesting information on how "inwardly" people are united with benevolent spirit beings.

o. What are the appropriate offerings to be made when people turn to them for help?

p. What stories and legends are there which highlight the intelligence and cunning of benevolent spirit beings?

3.4.7 What *permanent psychic dispositions* can be attributed to benevolent spirit beings?

☞ **Hint:**

It is obvious that the databank of permanent psychic dispositions pertaining to human beings elicited by questioning would be of advantage here.

a. Where are their permanent psychic dispositions located? (Do they have a "heart", "liver" etc.)?

b. What adjectives do informants use to describe the permanent psychic dispositions of benevolent spirit beings?

> ☞ **Hint:**
>
> As always it is important to collect as many contexts as possible originating from mother-tongue speakers.

c. What can annoy benevolent spirit beings?

d. Can they be reconciled again?

e. What preconditions must people fulfil so that they are prepared for reconciliation?

3.4.8 What *diseases* in people can be caused by benevolent spirit beings?

☞ **Hint:**

Although benevolent spirit beings have in general a positive attitude and are friendly towards people, situations can arise where they have occasion to inflict disease or illness on people. These can best be classified as "disciplinary measures".

    a. ***What social misdemeanours*** do benevolent spirit beings punish with illness or some form of calamity?

    b. What terms are used to describe this "punishment"?

    c. How serious or life-threatening can such diseases be for a person?

    d. ***Who*** undertakes ***what*** to bring about recovery form this disease?

3.4.9 What *"psychic conditions"* can benevolent spirit beings induce in people?

    a. Can benevolent spirit beings penetrate a person's body?

    b. What kinds of effects does a benevolent spirit being have on a person's *SEIC*?

    c. What effects are considered to be positive?

    d. How can ordinary people profit from the positive effects of benevolent spirit beings?

    e. Are there clues in the language to describe how benevolent spirit beings have a positive influence on a person's emotions and character?

    f. Can they also influence a person's intellect so that he or she has an experience of "enlightenment" (e.g. in exams etc.)?

    g. What rituals help to put a benevolent spirit being in such a good mood that a person experiences a heightened degree of intellectual capacity?

    h. What taboos have to be observed and kept so that a benevolent spirit being guarantees its support for particularly great intellectual capability?

3.4.10 Since benevolent spirit beings are very people-friendly, one of the places where they like to reside is close to or in the middle of people's habitation.

    a. Where else do benevolent spirit beings like to reside?

    b. Are these places described as "heavenly space"?

    c. Do benevolent spirit beings in such "heavenly spaces" live together in a community, in a settlement?

    d. What living conditions prevail there?

    e. Can one speak of the conditions as luxurious or paradisiacal (e.g. the land of Cockaigne)?

f. Do people use certain objects to secure the presence of benevolent spirit beings (mostly deceased relatives)?

g. Do these objects originate from the deceased relatives themselves?

h. How are these objects classified, i.e. what is the generic term for them?

☞ **Hint:**

Thiel writes that the Yansi in Africa call them "Ahnendinge" ("ancestor things") (in Käser 2014:127).

The Bemba in Zambia call them *Babenye*, the relics of an important person, one who has enjoyed special status during his life time (e.g. chiefs). The relics kept are usually items which were used by the person while alive (e.g. chair, bow and arrows, other weapons, ornaments etc.)

i. Where are those artefacts stored or kept?

☞ **Hint:**

Among the Bemba local chiefs have a hut *(ng'anda ya benye)*, in which such a person's relics are kept and guarded by a watchman *(muka benye)*.

j. Are there other places in the natural world which are regarded as favourite places where benevolent spirit beings reside?

k. Do these places have a special name?

l. Are there stories or happenings to do with these places which people recount?

m. Are they in people's immediate surroundings or further away from human settlements?

☞ **Hint:**

Benevolent spirit beings general reside in the "civilised" environment of people. Such an area can already terminate on the fringe of the village.

3.4.11 Among the benevolent spirit beings the *spirits of the deceased* are at the head of the hierarchy. In many ethnic groups which are considered to be *settled arable farmers* the biggest group of benevolent spirit beings is composed of the spirits of deceased relatives. This is why the following questions should be asked:

a. Are the spirits of the deceased regarded as benevolent spirit beings?

b. What are the characteristics of a benevolent spirit of the dead?

c. Does a benevolent spirit of the dead resemble that person in detail?

d. To what extent does a spirit of the dead perpetuate the physical features of the deceased person?

e. Are changes in the body which occurred during the person's lifetime visible on his or her benevolent spirit?

f. Can the spirit of the dead also be recognised by the clothing which the deceased wore when alive?

g. Is it possible for a benevolent spirit of the dead to assume other forms?

> ☞ **Hint:**
>
> Among the Bemba of Zambia pythons receive special regard. It is believed that deceased Bemba who have held office, including especially the Paramount Chief, can encounter people in the form of a python. This is why pythons are generally under protection.

h. What is the relationship of a benevolent spirit of the dead to its previous environment?

i. Does a benevolent spirit of the dead feel something akin to homesickness if it has been away from its familiar surroundings for a long time?

j. What feelings in particular reflect the homesickness of a benevolent spirit of the dead?

k. In terms of language to what extent do these feelings resemble the feelings that the living relatives experience among themselves?

l. To what extent do people perceive or reckon that benevolent spirits of the dead behave like living relatives?

m. What services or care can be expected as a matter of course from benevolent spirits of the dead?

n. Are benevolent spirits of the dead connected with a social group regarded by that group as members?

o. Can one say that benevolent spirits of the dead still regard themselves as members of their group?

p. To what degree do benevolent spirits of the dead perpetuate the group structure of their respective communities in the beyond?

3.4.12 Not all benevolent spirits of the dead receive special regard indiscriminately, but only those who had special status during their lives. These are held to be, in the exact sense of the term, *ancestral spirits*.

a. What knowledge or abilities must a person possess in order to be accorded special status?

b. Is it this knowledge or these abilities possessed by the person during life which later make it possible for that person to achieve the status of an ancestral spirit?

c. What is the term for ancestral spirits as opposed to other (benevolent) spirit beings?

d. What are the corresponding terms in the language for expressions like "our ancestors, forebears, father of the clan" etc.?

e. How is respect for an ancestral spirit expressed?

f. In linguistic formulae, in symbols, in special actions?

g. What actions directed against the community are avenged by ancestral spirits?

h. What are the words for "guilt", "be guilty", and "incur guilt"?

i. What are all the derivations and compounds?

j. What actions lead to the state of "being guilty"?

k. What consequences for a person result from the state of "being guilty"?

l. Can one in the same way speak of "incurring guilt" when the personal interests of ancestral spirits of the dead are not perceived or implemented?

Additional reading: **Käser** *Animism*, Chap. 9.

3.4.13 A special group of benevolent spirit beings consists of those which render *protection* and *support*. However, this group of benevolent spirit beings only plays a role in societies which know of no benevolent spirit beings which can be classified as ancestral spirits. This applies to non-residential groups, to nomadic peoples, to hunter-gatherer groups who secure their livelihood chiefly by means of hunting game or keeping livestock.

In *such societies* shamans enjoy a very high social status since they are perceived as the mediators between the visible, material world and the invisible, immaterial world.[9]

---

[9] The necessary distinction between settled and nomadic societies with reference to shamanism is still hardly or not at all sufficiently considered. In her article (published in Greifeld's

a. What is the word for shaman?

    ☞ **Hint:**

    In ethnographic studies of Bantu ethnic groups in Africa the healer (specialist in diseases) is often termed the shaman. However, the shaman should be differentiated from the *medium* (societies with veneration of ancestors).

    Additional reading: **Käser** *Animism*, Chap. 14 & 15.

b. How can one become a shaman (by succession, charisma, training etc.)?

c. Do the spirit beings choose a person or does that person choose the spirit being?

d. In what form (human, animal) do benevolent protective assistant spirits show themselves to the shaman (whether man or woman)?

e. Is there a hierarchy among the protective assistant spirits – i.e. is there a chief among all protective assistant spirits?

f. Have these protective assistant spirits ever possessed a body as a material counterpart?

g. Are the benevolent protective assistant spirits sexual beings, i.e. do they have male and female bodies?

h. In the particular ethnic group in which shamans are operating is there the notion that certain benevolent protective assistant spirits perpetuate the personality of deceased shamans?

i. Can a protective assistant spirit be regarded as the shaman's 'bodyguard'?

j. Is there a corresponding term in the language?

k. Are there terms referring to the assistant spirits as the shaman's 'counsellors'?

Ritual und Heilung and now in its third edition, and which could be considered as a standard work of introduction to the ethnology of medicine) Kutalek points out that certain elements (disease and the ancestors as accompanying transcendental beings) which are to be attributed to classical Siberian shamanism, are applied by many authors to African healing experts in terms of shamanism (2003:59). However, with regard to Africa this observation is of a general kind and ignores the necessary distinction made here (and in Käser). Elsewhere Greifeld und Schmidt note that "today shamanism is no longer so narrowly understood" as Elidade (1975) established with regard to North Asiatic Artic tribes (in Greifeld 2003:128). Certainly it is more than questionable whether a broadening of shamanism beyond its original framework can be undertaken. The being and importance of the shaman cannot be sought outside of his/her particular social environment (cf. Käser 2014:232).

l. Is there a notion which conveys that protective assistant spirits serve the shaman as a means of transport?

m. What designations or names does the shaman give to his protective assistant spirits?

n. Or to put the question another way: do the protective assistant spirits reveal their names themselves?

o. Does the shaman have a protective assistant spirit which is particularly close to him?

p. Does this protective assistant spirit bear the name of an animal?

q. Does it have this name because what this protective assistant spirit does relates to the nature of that animal?

r. Does the shaman have a female protective assistant spirit with which he cultivates a "love relationship"?

s. How many protective assistant spirits can a shaman gather around himself?

t. How can he acquire additional protective assistant spirits?

u. Can these spirit beings (protective assistant spirits) "inhabit" the body of the shaman?

v. Which body organ or location in the body is regarded as the "abode" of these spirit beings?

> ☞ **Hint:**
>
> The shaman Jungleman, a Yanomami in the Amazon, declares impressively that his protective assistant spirits reside in his chest. The word he uses in his language, *shabono,* is also the term for the traditional round huts the Yanomami live in.
>
> See: **Ritchie** 2000, *Spirit of the Rainforest.*

w. How can a shaman make contact with his protective assistant spirits?

x. What offences on the part of the shaman are punished by the protective assistant spirits?

y. What punishment do the protective assistant spirits inflict on a shaman who passes on his acquired knowledge to unauthorised persons?

z. What punishment must be expected by a shaman who disassociates himself from his protective assistant spirits?

3.4.14 Ethnic societies based fundamentally on animism recognise, among all the kinds of high-ranking benevolent spirit beings, one being which is superior to all the others. It is termed the *Supreme Being*.

a. What stories and legends are prevalent among the ethnic group you are working in?

b. How is the Supreme Being described with reference to his *sex*, *age* and *proximity* to the people?

c. Is the Supreme Being also seen as the creator of things (water, rain, fire, forest and plants) that belong to all humans without distinction?

d. In what ways is the Supreme Being venerated?

e. Are there 'hymns of praise' sung in the honour of the Supreme Being?

f. Do people also dance in his honour?

g. Are there proverbs containing statements about the Supreme Being?

> ☞ **Hint:**
>
> Such hymns and proverbs are often a rich source for discovering the notions held by an ethnic group about the Supreme Being.

h. Are there special occasions or times when honour is paid to the Supreme Being?

i. What basic emotional disposition is attributed to the Supreme Being?

j. What permanent psychic dispositions and intellectual abilities are ascribed to him?

k. What names are given to the Supreme Being?

> ☞ **Hint:**
>
> Language analysis can come up with interesting aspects and results here.

l. Is the Supreme Being married?

m. Does he have several wives?

n. Can he boast of numerous offspring?

o. To what extent are sons and daughters regarded as bringers of special technologies and implements for humans?

p. In what ways can people gain access to these technologies and implements (dream, a love relationship with a son or daughter of the Supreme Being, theft)?

q. Are there legends or myths in which one of the Supreme Being's offspring appears as the "black sheep of the family"?

r. How is his relationship to people described?

> ☞ **Hint:**
>
> In ethnological studies he is called the *trickster* (Käser 2014: 141).
>
> In many Bantu ethnic groups in Africa the trickster is the hare (in the Bemba language he is called *Kalulu*).

s. If there is such a being, what misdemeanours are blamed on him?

t. What permanent psychic dispositions are attributed to him, and what special physical features are peculiar to him?

u. What part does the Supreme Being play in the daily life of the people?

3.4.15 Where do benevolent spirit beings come from?

a. To what extent is it true that the largest group of benevolent spirit beings derive their origin from humans?

b. If yes, were they then already assigned to humans during their lifetime?

3.5 Searching for the Predominant or the most Prominent Spirit Double

As has already been mentioned, certain spirit beings are so closely united with a person that they are completely identical with that person and hence the two can be confused. Moreover ethnographic data shows that a person can be allocated several spirit beings. As such they accompany that person throughout life. However, among them all there is *one* benevolent spirit being displaying a profile which is essential to the concept of man held by ethnic groups.

This refers to that benevolent spirit being which not only accompanies a person during life, but also survives *the death* of the material body *and* perpetuates that person's personality after death.

This spirit being is termed the *spirit double* of the person. Because of this special feature such a spirit being has a prominent position among the other spirit beings or spirit doubles which accompany a person. Research should now be focused on which spirit double occupies this *superior* or *predominant* position.

The question is, which is the spirit being that survives the death of the body and *perpetuates the personality of the deceased individual!*

☞ **Hint:**

There are above all two features which distinguish this spirit double from all the other spirit doubles a person may have.

- Since a person can have several spirit doubles it is necessary to determine which of them perpetuates the ***personality*** of the deceased person. This spirit double is, as it were, that person's immortal second self. Only this prominent spirit double can normally become an ***ancestral spirit***.

Additional reading: **Käser** *Animism*, Chap. 11.

- At the same time this spirit double reveals itself as the being ***"whose experiences form the content of dreams"*** (Käser 2014:161).

3.5.1   How is this spirit being called?

☞ **Hint:**

Be mindful of linguistic nuances (see Chap. 3, 3.1)!

3.5.2   *When*, at *what moment* does the separation of this spirit being from the body of the dead person occur?

     a.   At the moment of a person's last breath?

     b.   After the *first* ritual of death has been performed?

     c.   After the burial of the body?

     d.   After the body has been burned?

     e.   After the proper disposal of the body according to traditional custom?

     f.   After *some* or *all* rituals of death (or the secondary burial) have taken place, their performance having followed traditional custom?

     g.   Or at a later time when the body already shows definite signs of decay?

3.5.3   Is this spirit double *benevolent* or *malevolent* as regards its being, or is it furnished with both qualities at the same time?

❑ **Important:**

Apart from ***benevolent*** and ***malevolent*** there are other adjectives which could be used to describe this spirit being (e.g. 'soft', 'whole', 'peaceful' or 'aggressive', 'hostile', 'cunning' etc.)

Additional reading: **Käser** *Animism*, Chap. 8 & 9.

As many contexts a possible should provide exact information, i.e. collect as many phrases as possible in the language of the people.

3.5.4 Does this spirit double (always insert the corresponding linguistic term) possess only *good* permanent psychic dispositions?

    a. Which good permanent psychic dispositions stand out in particular?

    b. How does this spirit double demonstrate these particularly positive permanent psychic dispositions to people?

3.5.6 Does this spirit double only have *negative* permanent psychic dispositions?

    a. Which negative permanent psychic dispositions stand out in particular?

    b. How does this spirit double demonstrate these particularly negative permanent psychic dispositions to people?

    ☞ **Hint:**

    The list of permanent psychic dispositions elicited to describe a person would be of use here.

3.5.7 Does this spirit double possess a blend of "good" and "bad" permanent psychic dispositions?

    a. What does this mixture of good and bad permanent psychic dispositions on the part of the spirit double mean in terms of a person's behaviour?

3.5.8 Can this spirit double itself influence its permanent psychic dispositions?

    a. If no, why not?

    b. If yes, how? (e.g. rituals, observance of cultural taboos etc.)

    ☞ **Important:**

    It is to be assumed that the collection of data on permanent psychic dispositions applicable to spirit doubles *only* contains *good* attributes / traits.

    This means that according to its character this *being is a benevolent spirit double*.

3.5.9 Does this spirit double have a sex?

    a. Is this spirit double of the male sex if the person with whose body it was conjoined is or was a man?

    b. Is this spirit double of the female sex if the person with whose body it was conjoined is or was a woman?

    c. Is this spirit double androgynous (does it possess both male and female sex characteristics)?

    d. Is this spirit double without sex (in a biological sense)?

3.5.10 Is this spirit double able to be aware of bodily sensations?

    a. Is it able to feel heat or cold?

    b. Is it able to feel pain?

    c. Is it able to have a feeling of hunger or thirst?

    d. Can it be sexually aroused?

    e. If yes, what can lead to sexual stimulation?

        ☞ **Hint:**

        Here one must be careful to be culturally sensitive. Above all make sure whether it is appropriate for a man to question a woman about this, or vice versa!

    f. Is there evidence that it possesses body temperature?

        ☞ **Hint:**

        The databank drawn up for persons can also be very useful here.

        Can all human bodily sensations also apply to this prominent spirit double?

        These questions will certainly lead to interesting results and insights. Certain bodily sensations will assuredly *not* be applicable to this being.

        One should be sure to register those particular bodily sensations which can be applied to this spirit double!

        This should enable one to deduce the important features of the being which survives the death of the body and perpetuates the personality of the deceased person.

3.5.11 Does this spirit double have feelings and emotions and does it have the capacity to show them?

☞ **Hint:**

If yes, then it is quite certain that it has its *own **SEIC*** and hence independence *as a person*!

  a. In what ways does it demonstrate feelings and emotions?

  b. How does a happy and contented spirit double influence the community to which its individual ("human companion" **Badenberg** 1999/2002:93) belongs?

  c. How do positive feelings become noticeable in this spirit double?

  d. How do they manifest themselves?

  e. Would it cause the person to whom it is assigned to have exactly the same feelings and emotions as itself?

  f. In what situations would this happen?

  g. What happens when it senses anger or trouble?

  h. What does it mean for the individual if his or her spirit double experiences negative emotions?

3.5.12 It is a good idea to draw on the databank of feelings and emotions and apply all the terms to the being that survives the death of the body.

☞ **Hint:**

It would be best to start with the positive feelings and emotions and only after that to analyse the list of negative feelings and emotions.

After this is done a further area can be opened up. The following question will gain access to this new sphere.

3.5.13 Is this spirit double which survives the death of the body *and* perpetuates the personality of the deceased person also the being which departs from the body of its person during a dream?

❑ **Important:**

If yes, then this being can also be designated the *DREAM-EGO*.

One can then be sure to have identified the *predominant* or *prominent spirit double*. Only this *benevolent, prominent* spirit double is the person's *dream-ego* and as a rule can become an *ancestral spirit*.

In cultures shaped by an agricultural environment (like the Bemba of Zambia, for example), the spirit double that survives the death of the body can also be identical with the being which perpetuates the personality of the deceased person, and also the dream-ego.

In some ethnic groups people can have up to 50 different spirit doubles. However, and this is crucial, only *one* of them is the dream-ego (i.e. dreams are the experiences of the dream-ego which it communicates to the person it belongs to in dreams).

It is recommended to draw up further lists of questions about the *feelings*, *emotions*, *permanent psychic dispositions* and *intellectual abilities* of the dream-ego.

This will help to broaden and further consolidate the data on the nature of its *SEIC*.

It will make things considerably easier for the informant if one works with the relevant term for spirit double and *dream-ego*!

3.6   The Dream-ego and the Name of a Person

3.6.1   Is the dream-ego in any way connected with the name of a person?

a. How does the selection of the name of a person happen?

[Through particular rituals, special actions and events or *circumstances*: e.g. a child born on a Friday is called "Friday" etc. On the other hand a particular characteristic can lead to the naming: e.g. if the child is born bald, physically handicapped or is unusually hairy or carries birthmarks].

b. Do dreams have an influence on the selection of the name?

c. Does the dream ego reveal to the parents or close relatives in a dream what name they should choose?

d. Does the dream-ego play any part at all in the naming of a child?

e. Is the moment of naming the same moment in which the dream-ego is assigned to a person?

f. If not, when can one assume that a person takes possession of a dream-ego?

g. Does a person receive more than one dream-ego?

h. How can a person receive more than one dream-ego?

⇨ **Example:**

The Bemba of Zambia believe that a person can receive either a new dream-ego through a new name or a further dream-ego through an additional name. Furthermore it is possible to take over the prominent spirit double (*umupashi* = dream-ego) of another person.

This notion is based on one of the principles of the culture, that each person who dies **must** obtain a successor among the living.

For example, when a child dies it is usual for the grandparents to take over its dream-ego (*umupashi*). However, when a married man dies a successor (*impyani*) has to be found for him, and he then has to marry the widow of the deceased.

The successor retains his own dream-ego and takes over *umupashi* of the deceased. He can then be called by his own name and/or by the name of the deceased.

Additional reading: **Badenberg** 1999/2002, Chap. 5.

3.6.2   **Some ethnic groups give their members more than a single name. As a rule, though, the real or secret name can only be known by *one* other person in the group. This knowledge give this person absolute power over him.**

☞ **Hint:**

This is the case among the Motilone Indians, an ethnic group of Venezuela in South America (see Olson 1995:114).

   a. Would the knowledge of the real name of a person in the ethnic group you are working in have an influence on the person and/or the dream-ego?

   b. Under what circumstances would a person divulge their real name to another person?

      ☞ **Hint:**

      For example a ritual which cements a friendship that is to be valid for life. Olson reports that among the Motilone pacts are sealed between families and individuals. A pact between two individuals makes them brothers in the fullest sense (Olson 1995:112-113).

   c. In what way [what action is carried out, or under what conditions] would someone reveal their real name to someone else?

3.7   The Dream-ego – its Origin

3.7.1   Where do dream-egos come from?

   a. Are they pre-existent?

   b. Is there a place within the tribal territory which they occupy, claim or reside in?

   c. Is there a place in "heaven" or the underworld which they occupy, claim or reside in?

   d. Are dream-egos being "born"?

   e. Are the mothers of dream-egos female spirit beings?

   f. Or are they born by mortal mothers?

   g. Can they suffer 'death'?

   h. Are they part of some sort of 'family'?

   ☞ **Hint:**

Explanations that concern the origin of dream-egos are manifold and are often mere assumptions.

Additional reading: **Käser** *Animism*, Chap. 11.

In many Bantu African groups the dream-ego of a deceased relative re-assigns itself to a child or young person.

   ⇨ **Example:**

Among the Bemba of Zambia the dream-egos of people who have demonstrated an exemplary life are re-assigned to a new-born baby with the name of the deceased.

Hence maintaining the integrity of the family history means guarding and preserving the 'good name', so that the dream-ego is ready to be recalled for future generations.

However, this has nothing really to do with ***belief in reincarnation*** or ***animistic recycling***.

Additional reading: **Käser** *Animism*, Chap. 11 and **Badenberg** 2008, Chap. 2.

3.7.2   Can a person see his own dream-ego?

   a. If yes, when and under what circumstances can this happen?

   b. How would it happen?: in dreams or in some kind of apparition?

3.7.3 If not, who is able to see the dream-ego of a person?

    a. Any person?

    b. Only special persons (seer, medium)?

    c. Are there particular times when the dream-ego can be seen (e.g. during a festival, at full moon, at special moments in life etc.)?

3.7.4 Is a special event or ritual required for a person to be able to see his or her own dream-ego?

    a. Does the observance of the required ritual 'force' the dream-ego, as it were, to grant or fulfil the wishes or objectives of that person?

    b. Are other additional offerings required to enable the dream-ego to be seen?

    c. If yes, who determines what offerings are necessary?

3.7.5 Can the persons involved choose the offerings themselves?

    a. If not, are the offerings determined or prescribed by the dream-ego?

    b. How, in what way and to whom are the demands communicated?

3.8 The Dream-ego and Dreams

3.8.1 Is it possible to see the dream-ego in a dream?

    a. If yes, does the dream-ego bear *corporeal marks* that are absolutely *identical* to corporeal marks of the living person?

    b. In case the dream-ego shows itself, makes itself visible, does it prefer to do so wearing *special clothes*, *special regalia* (e.g. shining white, European or traditional fashion)?

    c. Who is able to see the dream-ego of another person?

    d. Is this possible while awake or does it only happen while dreaming or being in a state of trance?

3.8.2 Does the dream-ego travel/go on a journey while a person is asleep?

    a. If yes, which places, localities does it frequently visit or are its favourites?

    b. What would or could happen if a person asleep were be suddenly and forcefully aroused from sleep, while the dream-ego is still wandering about or on a journey?

    c. Are the pictures, the episodes a person sees in a dream actually the adventures of the dream-ego while on a journey?

☞ **Important:**

Although the contents of dreams – judging by what is still remembered after waking up – are the experiences of the dream-ego, are they recounted *not* in the second person, but in the first person? ("**I** have dreamed")!

This is a case of classic cognitive dissonance, and one should not allow oneself to be confused by it.

a. Are there other ways in which the dream-ego conveys messages to the people to which it is assigned?

b. If yes, does the majority of messages relate to (important) events to do with the future of that person?

(This would mean that the dream-ego is the agent who opens "a window into the future").

☞ **Hint:**

One can assume that there are various categories of dreams. It is possible that there may be "normal" dreams (the expression the language uses is important here!).

'Normal' dreams usually arise from particular events or strong desires a person has.

⇨ **Example:**

Among the Bemba in Zambia normal dreams are called *ifiloto fya matontonkanya* = the dreams of the thoughts.

In addition there could be a category of dreams which are attributed exclusively to the dream-ego. (Here, too, keep a lookout for the expression in the language!)

In Bemba these dreams are termed *ifiloto fya ku umupashi,* the dreams which are the gift of one's spirit double.

These dreams are special and valuable because they contain either the experiences of the dream-ego or messages concerning the person's future.

Additional reading: **Badenberg** 1999/2002, Chap. 5 and **Käser** *Animism*, Chap. 12.

3.9   The Dream-ego – Loss or Absence and Illness

3.9.1   In what way is the dream-ego related to the body of a person?

a. Does it predominantly reside *inside* the body of a person?

b. Does it usually reside *outside* the body of a person?

c. What kind of feelings or fears do people have whose dream-ego usually resides outside the body?

d. Does one have to fear it is roaming about freely without hinting at its whereabouts?

e. To what danger are persons exposed to if the dream-ego is absent for a longer period of time?

f. Is there linguistic evidence that proves the dream-ego has got a (profound) sense of responsibility or sense of duty?

g. Is there some kind of idea which suggests that the dream-ego avoids closeness to the body because of a row or a quarrel it had with its 'human companion'?

3.9.2   Is it possible to lose one's dream-ego?

a. What could be reasons for a person to lose his dream-ego?

b. What is the phrase in which the loss of one's dream-ego is expressed?

☞ **Hint:**

Collect as many sentences, expressions or sayings as possible which stem from indigenous speakers.

c. How, in what way does the loss of one's dream-ego manifest itself?

☞ **Important:**

In many cultures the temporary loss or transitory absence of the dream-ego signifies a limitation of the body's ability to function properly. Collect contexts in the language!

In some societies the temporary absence of the dream-ego has a tiring effect on the body and makes it go to sleep.

Additional reading: **Käser** *Animism*, Chap. 11.

Reinhard Ablaßmeier has an account of the illness *quedada* or *huaytay* in Peru which, as he terms it, is caused by "loss of the soul". People "lose energy, complain of fatigue ..., increasingly withdraw themselves, ... often lie for days in bed. At night the illness causes them to start up in fright, scream, moan and weep." (in Greifeld 2003:27).

It is to be noted that Ablaßmeier defines the two terms *ánimo* and *espiritu* as being equivalent to soul (in Greifeld 2003:27).

To be precise one should in all probability speak of a spirit double. Whether it is indeed the dream-ego would depend on closer research.

At all events it is clear how easily European-Western concepts (here that of the soul) can be applied to complex indigenous systems. It is likewise clear how little headway the concept of the spirit double or dream-ego has made till now in ethnographic publications (including cultural anthropology and medical ethnology).

    d. To what dangers are persons who have lost their dream-ego exposed?

    e. How can a dream-ego which has absented itself be recovered again?

    f. Can it indeed be recovered at all?

    g. Who can help someone who has suffered the loss of the dream-ego?

3.9.3 Which are the main functions of the body which suffer loss of efficiency when the dream-ego is *absent*?

    a. Is this condition referred to as an *illness*?

    a. Is there a *category* of illnesses or diseases which are caused by the absence of the dream-ego?

   ☞ **Important:**

If yes, collect the *terms* for these illnesses or diseases, *analyse them linguistically*, and record the *process of the disease* and *methods of treatment*.

3.9.4 Is it possible to 'capture' a person's dream-ego, 'set a trap for it' or 'steal' it?

    a. What could be the reason for a person wanting to 'capture', 'steal' or 'set a trap' for someone else's dream-ego?

     ☞ **Hint:**

Try to find the word for this act. In Bemba thinking one can indeed 'capture' or 'set a trap' for the dream-ego.

Hunter-gatherers probably also have a words for it related to their way of life.

    b. What does a person have to do in order to 'set a trap', 'capture' or 'steal' someone's dream-ego?

    c. What can a person do to guard against it being stolen, captured, or a trap being set for it?

    d. Does 'capturing' or 'setting a trap' for a dream-ego mean that it is barred from a certain *place* or *village* or can be held imprisoned there?

    e. Or does it mean that the dream-ego can or has to be held captive in a *closed* or *sealed* container (e.g. a container with a lid, a box with a lid, a drum, a jar etc.)?

    f. Can the dream-ego be released from its imprisonment or banishment?

    g. If yes, what has to be done to achieve the release (rituals, offerings etc.)?

    h. Can the dream-ego be 'banished' or 'held captive' for ever?

    i. What happens to a person whose dream-ego has been 'captured', 'trapped' or 'stolen'?

    j. What symptoms are characteristic of a person whose dream-ego is being 'held captive'?

    k. Where can a person's dream-ego be held captive?

    l. How long can a person's dream-ego be 'held captive' without that person suffering harm?

3.10 The Dream-ego and the Human Body

3.10.1 How is the dream-ego connected to the living person, what is the relationship between the two?

    a. Is it linked to the person's breath?

    b. To the man's semen?

    c. To his blood?

        ☞ **Hint:**

        The notion that the dream-ego is connected with a man's breath or semen is almost certainly not relevant here. Such notions are probably only met with in the Indo-Germanic speaking world. Nevertheless the question can or should be put.

3.10.2 Does the dream-ego have a preference for a special location in the body or a particular organ of the body?

    a. If yes, ask why this particular location is preferred?

   b. If this pert of the body is causing the person problems (e.g. pain, unwell feelings), does this imply that the dream-ego is present or absent or carrying out some other activity?

3.11 The Dream-ego and the *SEIC* of a Person

3.11.1 Is the dream-ego of a person/child involved in the education and upbringing of this person/child?

   a. If yes, how or in what way?

   b. Do people, who think the dream-ego does take positive action in the upbringing of their child, adjust to in in their own principles and methods of education?

   c. For example, in the way children are disciplined?

   d. Do parents employ corporal punishment in the upbringing of their children?

   e. If so, often, mildly, extremely rarely, only if absolutely necessary or never at all?

3.11.2 Is the restraint in the use of corporal punishment in a child's upbringing derived from the notion that it could amount to interference in what the dream-ego is achieving in the development of the child's personality?

3.11.3 What do parents do if their child is behaving badly or, which is far worse, when it is noticeable that it is developing ways of behaving which are contrary to cultural norms?

3.11.4 Do the parents turn to the dream-ego? Do they invoke its support through rituals in word (prayers) and deed (offerings), in order to bring about a change in the child's behaviour?

   ☞ **Hint:**

In Bemba there is evidence for this in the language. Invoking the dream-ego (*umupashi*) can contain notions implying that the child's *SEIC* is to be "*bent straight*" again or "*adjusted*", so that it can *think clearly* again and behave *properly*, i.e. *according to the norms*.

Additional reading: **Badenberg** 2008, Chap. 2.

3.12 The Dream-ego and a Person's Conduct

3.12.1 Does a person's way of life have a direct influence on his dream-ego?

   a. Does a person's bad way of life (which is in a sense a reflection of his character) cause the *SEIC* of the dream-ego to be harmed?

b. Does a bad way of life cause the dream-ego to distance itself from that person?

c. Does a ***permanently*** bad way of life bring ruin both to the person's *SEIC* and the *SEIC* of the dream-ego?

> ☞ **Hint:**
>
> If yes, make sure to record the language expression describing this 'process of disintegration'.
>
> In connection with this condition of ruination the Bemba speak of *"ukonaula umupashi"* or *"ukonaika umupashi"* – complete destruction of the *SEIC* of the Dream-egos.

Additional reading: **Badenberg** 1999/2002, Chap. 5.

3.12.2 Does the dream-ego of a person pose danger to the relatives of the deceased?

a. What could be the reasons why the dream-ego of a deceased relative would pose a danger to them?

b. How can relatives protect themselves from a perceived danger the dream-ego of the deceased could pose to them?

3.12.3 Does the dream-ego of a dead person long to cause harm to the *enemies* of the deceased?

a. How, in what way could it cause harm to them?

b. For how long would it keep on causing harm to them?

c. Until the enemies so to speak "surrender"?

d. Until the dream-ego feels it has had enough revenge?

3.12.4 Are the dream-egos of dead ancestors (ancestor spirits in the true sense) concerned about the living?

a. How, in what way would they show their concern for them?

b. How, in what way would they never at all show their concern for them?

c. What are the reasons that could lead to a situation where they would cut-off their support, their concern for the living?

3.12.5 Do dream-egos of deceased ancestors fight for the well-being of the members of the group/clan?

a. Is it necessary on the part of the living members of the group/clan to specifically call on the dream-egos of deceased members for help?

    b. Do dream-egos of ancestors intervene on their own, that is, do they maintain their own agenda (e.g. pick time and action at their convenience)?

3.12.6 Are the living members of the social group able to call their dead warriors for help, that is, to enlist a "spiritual army" and help them fight their cause?

    a. If yes, how?

    b. If no, why not or what could hinder them from offering their help and intervention?

3.12.7 Does a family clan or an extended family have one common dream-ego for all its members?

    a. Are the dream-egos of a family clan or an extended family related to one another?

    b. In what way are they related to one another?

    c. Do relationships that exist between dream-egos during the life time of a person continue even after death?

    d. Can a person exchange his dream-ego for the dream-ego of another person while they are both alive?

    e. If so, under what circumstances might this be possible?

    f. Are the dream-egos of all people equal?

    g. Are there differences between the dream-egos of:

- Africans and Europeans?
- Indians and Africans?
- Japanese, Chinese and Africans?
- Indians und Europeans?
- Asians and Indians?

    h. Would the differences that exist between the dream-egos of different ethnic groups also count as the principle reason why there are differences between different ethnic groups?

3.13 Dream-ego, Shadow, and Mirror Image

Detailed questioning on this topic is an essential part of investigating an ethnic group's concept of man. In the relevant literature shadow and mirror image are frequently termed the *shadow soul* of the person. The origin of this lies in the fact that a person's reflection in the mirror, and the shadow one casts, are sometimes also the term for one's dream-ego.

By more precise study of the terms 'shadow', 'shadow image', 'reflection' or 'mirror image' it is possible to discover the commonalities and differences. Hence it is essential to engage in linguistic research!

3.13.1 What is the word for shadow?

a. Is the word for shadow and dream-ego identical?

b. Can the word for shadow be equally applied to humans, animals, objects, and plants?

c. Do people differentiate in terms of language use or vocabulary between the shadow of a tree and the shadow of a human being?

d. Is there a profound linguistic distinction between 'casting a shadow' and a place/spot 'in the shade'?

    ☞ **Hint:**

    The Bemba in Zambia distinguish between *icinshingwa (shadow)* and *icintelelwe (shade)*, the spot that enjoys the protection against the heat of the sun.

    (This is true also of English, of course, although not of German).

    Additional reading: **Badenberg** 1999/2002, Chap. 6.

    It will be necessary to gather as many sentences or contexts as possible in which both words are used. Indigenous speakers need to be consulted.

e. How does one say: "I will sit in the shade of a tree and enjoy its protection from the heat of the sun".

f. How to people react toward a person who steps (intentionally or unintentionally) on their shadow?

e. Are there fears that someone could use the soil on which a person's shadow has fallen to cast a shadow spell?

f. What happens in the following situation: someone collects the soil on which the shadow of a person is falling or has fallen. Can this action have an influence on this person's dream-ego?

i. Even more serious, can a person's dream-ego be 'captured' and then also 'held captive' through that person's shadow?

3.13.2 What is the word for mirror image?

3.13.3 How are mirror reflections expressed in language phrases?

3.13.4 How does one say: "I see my image reflected in the mirror."

3.13.5 Or: "Someone is looking at himself in the mirror."

3.13.6 Or: "The sun is casting a reflection on the water."

☞ **Hint:**

Additional reading: **Käser** *Animism,* Chap. 11.

3.13.7 What is the word for a two-dimensional image, e.g. a copy?

⇨ **Example:**

The Bemba in Zambia call a two-dimensional picture *Icikope* (borrowed from the English word *copy*).

See **Badenberg** 1999/2002, Chap. 6.

3.13.8 In what contexts is this word used?

☞ **Hint:**

Collect as many sentences, expressions or sayings as possible which stem from indigenous speakers as possible.

3.13.9 What is the word for a three-dimensional image, e.g. "to bear the image of another person; to resemble another Person"?

⇨ **Example:**

A three-dimensional image is in Bemba called *Icata. Icata* can be applied to humans as well as to animals.

"Iyi imbushi naikwata icata nga ilyaikalamba" – this goat has the same image as the big one, the grown one = this goat is identical to the big/grown goat.

"Uyu mwana alikwata icata candi" – this child has got my image = this child takes after me in all aspects (even personality traits).

☞ **Hint:**

Important for Bible Translation work: man as the image of God etc.

3.13.10 In what contexts is this word used?

☞ **Hint:**

Collect as many sentences, expressions or sayings as possible which stem from indigenous speakers as possible.

Chapter 4
Support and Examples

This chapter provides some guidance on the extensive meanings of anthropological key terms in the Hebrew Old Testament. This is meant to support research in connection with biblical findings. In addition two concrete examples are set out to illustrate the importance of researching the concept of man with regard to Bible translation work.

4.0 The Domain *nefesh* (נֶפֶשׁ)

(Based on Wolff 1984:25-48)

Nefesh: primary meaning ***Gullet, Throat***

Psa 107:9	The thirsty and the hungry *nefesh* (throat)
Pro 10:3	*nefesh* (throat)
Isa 5:14	*nefesh* (gullet, throat)
Hab 2:5	*nefesh* (gullet, throat)

Nefesh meaning ***Breathing***

Gen 35:18	As she breathed (*nafsah*) her last ...
1 Ki 17:22	The LORD heard Elijah's cry, and the boy's *nefesh* returned to him = his breath returned to him
Job 11:20	Their hope will become a dying *nefesh* = a dying gasp
Job 41:13	His breath (*nafso*) sets coals ablaze
Jer 2:24	Sniffing (*nafsah*) the wind in her craving
Jer 15:9	The mother of seven ... will breathe (*nafsah*) her last

Nefesh meaning the ***Neck***

1 Sa 28:9	Why have you set a snare around my *nafsi* (neck) ...
Psa 105:18	His *nefesh* (neck) was put in irons
Jer 4:10	..."when a knife is at our *nefesh*" = at our throats/necks

Nefesh: ***Desire, Craving, Striving, Pursuit*** or ***Longing***

Psa 35:26	Man becomes the *nefesh* of his rivals = he became the object of their desire, their longing.
Prov 13:2b	the craving and desire of those who break trust.

Nefesh as **the desire** as such, **the human impulse** as the essence of desiring

2 Sa 3:21	that you may be king, according to your *nefesh* = according to your desire
Prov 21:10	the *nefesh* of the godless crave ... indicates clearly the desire of the godless.
Isa 26:9	the desire, the longing that I covet, is God.

Nefesh as the **seat of emotions and psychic dispositions**

Exo 23:9	here one could for the first time translate *nefesh* as soul, or the term psyche (*SEIC*) would be just as good.
Jdg 18:25	the *nefesh* is outraged, because it has been insulted
1 Sa 1:10	the *nefesh* is bitter because of childlessness
2 Sa 5:8	the *nefesh* hates
2 Ki 4:21	the *nefesh* is troubled because of illness
Job 19:2	*nefesh* as the organ that empathises with the one in need
Psa 6:3	the *nefesh* is afraid
Psa 19:8b	the *nefesh* is joyous and happy
Psa 31:8	the *nefesh* is suffering distress
Psa 35:8	the *nefesh* is joyful and gives praises to Yahweh
Psa 35:25b	the *nefesh* acquired what she desired
Psa 42:6, 12; 43:5	the *nefesh* is despairing and disquieted
Psa 78:18b	the *nefesh* desires, is craving for
Psa 131:2a	the *nefesh* is content and still
Isa 53:11	the *nefesh* is suffering hardship
Jer 4:31	the *nefesh* is exhausted and feels defenceless
Jer 12:7	the *nefesh* loves
Jer 13:21	The *nefesh* feels sorrow and weeps
Jona 2:8	The *nefesh* feels weak and despondent

Nefesh meaning **Life as such**

| Lev 17:11 | "the *nefesh* of the flesh" = the life [of the flesh], it is in the blood |
| Lev 24:17f | "if a man slays a *nefesh*" = takes life |

Lev 24:18b	*"nefesh* for *nefesh"* = life for life
Deu 12:23	"The blood, that is the *nefesh"* = the life
Pro 8:35f	"Whoever fails to find me harms his *nefesh"* = his life
Pro 19:8	"whoever acquires knowledge and understanding, he loves his *nefesh"* = his life
Psa 30:4	"Yahweh, you have brought up my *nefesh*" = my life from the underworld
Job 2:4	the Satan knows: a man will give all for a *nefesh* = for his life

Nefesh: Synonym for **person, individual, being**

Gen 2:7	describes man as *nefesh hajja.* Only after God gave man breath or enabled him to breathe does he become a living being, a living person, a living individual.
Lev 17:10	God turns his face against the *nefesh* = the person who sheds blood
Lev 20:6	the *nefesh* = person who turns to spirits of the dead
Lev 23:30	every *nefesh* = every person who does any kind of work on this day shall be blotted out from among the people.
Num 6:8	speaks of a *nefesh met,* contrasting it with a *nefesh hajja.* This is not to be thought of as a "dead soul" or a person who has been killed, **but** as a deceased person, a dead individual, a body or corpse, a dead form.

Nefesh: as *Personal Pronoun* – as Synonym for *I*

Gen 12:8	"Say you are my sister, so that I will be treated well for your sake and my *nefesh* will be spared because of you." Abraham does not mean that his soul will stay alive, but that he himself ("I") wants to stay alive. Better translation: "so that my life will be spared because of you."
Gen 19:19f	"… sparing my *nefesh*! (*me*); … then my *nefesh*! (*I*) will be spared."
1 Ki 20:32	"Please let my *nefesh* live!" = "let *me* live!"
Jdg 16:30	Samson cried: "Let my *nefesh* die with the Philistines" = "Let *me* die with the Philistines"
Num 23:10	Balaam said: "Let my *nefesh* die the death of the righteous!" = "May *I* die the death of the righteous!"

Psa 54:4	"Surely God is my help, the Lord is the one who sustains my *nefesh* " = sustains **me**. Gen 27:4, 19, 25, 31 is interesting. Four times during his blessing Jacob mentions his *nefesh*.
Gen 27:4	... so that my *nefesh* may bless you before I die = so that **I** may bless you before I die!
Gen 27:19	... that your *nefesh* may bless me! = that **you** may bless me!
Gen 27:25	... see above!
Gen 27:31	... see above!

Translating *nefesh* in the blessing passage of Gen 27 with "soul" is totally inadequate, since it can easily make one think of some special energy and capacity of the soul. The next step, towards magical notions of the "soul", is then not far away.

Unfortunately the Luther Bible of 1984 has used 'soul' to translate every occurrence. English translations such as the NIV and the New Revised Standard Version are better here. Both versions have removed "soul" and put the appropriate personal pronoun instead.

4.1 *Nefesh* (נֶפֶשׁ) in the Hebrew Bible (References)

Gen   1:20, 21, 24, 30; 2:7, 19; 9:4, 5, 10, 12, 15, 16; 12:5, 13; 14:21; 17:14;
19:17, 19, 20; 23:8; 27:4, 19, 25, 31; 32:31; 34:3, 8; 35:18; 36:6; 37:21;
42:21; 44:30; 46:15, 18, 22, 25-27; 49:6

Exo   1:5; 4:19; 12:4, 15, 16, 19; 15:9; 16:16; 21:23, 30; 23:9; 30:12, 15, 16;
31:14

Lev   2:1; 4:2, 27; 5:1, 2, 4, 15, 17, 21; 7:18, 20, 21, 25, 27; 11:10, 43, 44, 46;
16:29, 31; 17:10-12, 14, 15; 18:29; 19:8, 28; 20:6, 25; 21:1, 11; 22:3, 4,
6, 11; 23:27, 29, 30, 32; 24:17, 18; 26:11, 15, 16, 30, 43; 27:2

Num   5:2, 6; 6:6, 11; 9:6, 7, 10, 13; 11:6; 15:27, 28, 30, 31; 17:3; 19:11, 13,
18, 20, 22; 21:4, 5; 23:10; 29:7; 30:3, 5-14; 31:19, 28, 35, 40, 46, 50;
35:11, 15, 30, 31

Deu   4:9, 15, 29; 6:5; 10:12, 22; 11:13, 18; 12:15, 20, 21, 23; 13:4, 7; 14:26;
18:6; 19:6, 11, 21; 21:14; 22:26; 23:25; 24:6, 7, 15; 26:16; 27:25; 28:65;
30:2, 6, 10

Jos   2:13, 14; 9:24; 10:28, 30, 32, 35, 37, 39; 11:11; 20:3, 9; 22:5; 23:11, 14

Jdg   5:18, 21; 9:17; 10:16; 12:3; 16:16, 30; 18:25

Ruth   4:15

1 Sa   1:10, 15, 26; 2:16, 33, 35; 17:55; 18:1, 3; 19:5, 11; 20:1, 3, 4, 17; 22:2,
22, 23; 23:15, 20; 24:12; 25:26, 29; 26:21, 24; 28:9, 21; 30:6

2 Sa   1:9; 3:21; 4:8, 9; 5:8; 11:11; 14:7, 14, 19; 16:11; 17:8; 18:13; 19:6;
23:17

1 Ki   1:12, 29; 2:4, 23; 3:11; 8:48; 11:37; 17:21, 22; 19:2-4, 10, 14; 20:31, 32,
39, 42

2 Ki   1:13, 14; 2:2, 4, 6; 4:27, 30; 7:7; 9:15; 10:24; 12:5; 23:3, 25

1 Ch   5:21; 11:19; 22:19; 28:9

2 Ch   1:11; 6:38; 15:12; 34:31

Est   4:13; 7:3,7; 8:11; 9:16, 31

Job   2:4, 6; 3:20; 6:7, 11; 7:11, 15; 9:21; 10:1; 11:20; 12:10; 13:14; 14:22;
16:4; 18:4; 19:2; 21:25; 23:13; 24:12; 27:2, 8; 30:16, 25; 31:30, 39;
32:2; 33:18, 20, 22, 28, 30; 36:14; 41:13

Psa   3:3; 6:4, 5; 7:3, 6; 10:3; 11:1, 5; 13:3; 16:10; 17:9, 13; 19:8; 22:21, 30;
23:3; 24:4; 25:1, 13, 20; 26:9; 27:12; 30:4; 31:8, 10, 14; 33:19, 20; 34:3,
23; 35:3, 4, 7, 9, 12, 13, 17, 25; 38:13; 40:15; 41:3, 5; 42:2, 3, 5-7, 12;
43:5; 44:26; 49:9, 16, 19; 54:5, 6; 55:19; 56:7, 14; 57:2, 5, 7; 59:4; 62:2,
6; 63:2, 6, 9, 10; 66:9, 16; 69:2, 11, 19; 70:3; 71:10, 13, 23; 72:13, 14;

74:19; 77:3; 78:18, 50; 84:3; 86:2, 4, 13, 14; 88:4, 15; 89:49; 94:17, 19, 21; 97:10; 103:1, 2, 22; 104:1, 35; 105:18, 22; 106:15; 107:5, 9, 18, 26; 109:20, 31; 116:4, 7, 8; 119:20, 25, 28, 81, 109, 129, 167, 175; 120:2, 6; 121:7; 123:4; 124:4, 5, 7; 130:5, 6; 131:2; 138:3; 139:14; 141:8; 142:5, 8; 143:3, 6, 8, 11, 12; 146:1

Pro 1:18, 19; 2:10; 3:22; 6:16, 26, 30, 32; 7:23; 8:36; 10:3; 11:17, 25, 30; 12:10; 13:2-4, 8, 19, 25; 14:10, 25; 15:32; 16:17, 24, 26; 18:7; 19:2, 8, 15, 16, 18; 20:2; 21:10,23; 22:5, 23, 25; 23:2, 7, 14; 24:12, 14; 25:13, 25; 27:7, 9; 28:17, 25; 29:10, 17, 24; 31:6

Ecc 2:24; 4:8; 6:2, 3, 7, 9; 7:28

Son 1:7; 3:1-4; 5:6; 6:12

Isa 1:14; 3:9, 20; 5:14; 10:18; 15:4; 19:10; 26:8, 9; 29:8; 32:6; 38:15, 17; 42:1; 43:4; 44:20; 46:2; 47:14; 49:7; 51:23; 53:10-12; 55:2, 3; 56:11; 58:3, 5, 10, 11; 61:10; 66:3

Jer 2:24, 34; 3:11; 4:10, 19, 30, 31; 5:9, 29; 6:8, 16; 9:8; 11:21; 12:7; 13:17; 14:19; 15:1, 9; 17:21; 18:20; 19:7, 9; 20:13; 21:7, 9; 22:25, 27; 26:19; 31:12, 14, 25; 32:41; 34:16, 20, 21; 37:9; 38:2, 16, 17, 20; 39:18; 40:14, 15; 42:20; 43:6; 44:7, 14, 30; 45:5; 46:26; 48:6; 49:37; 50:19; 51:6, 14, 45; 52:29, 30

Lam 1:11, 16, 19; 2:12, 19; 3:17, 20, 24, 25, 51, 58; 5:9

Eze 3:19, 21; 4:14; 7:19; 13:18-20; 14:14, 20; 16:5, 27; 17:17; 18:4, 20, 27; 22:25, 27; 23:17, 18, 22, 28; 24:21, 25; 25:6, 15; 27:13, 31; 32:10; 33:5, 6, 9; 36:5; 47:9

Hos 4:8; 9:4

Amo 2:14, 15; 6:8

Jona 1:14; 2:6, 8; 4:3, 8

Mic 6:7; 7:1, 3

Hab 2:4, 5, 10

Hag 2:13

Zec 11:8

4.2   *Ruach* (רוּחַ) in the Hebrew Bible (References)

Gen   1:2; 3:8; 6:3, 17; 7:15, 22; 8:1; 26:35; 41:8, 38; 45:27

Exo   6:9; 10:13, 19; 14:21; 15:8, 10; 28:3; 31:3; 35:21, 3

Num   5:14, 30; 11:17, 25, 26, 29, 31; 14:24; 16:22; 24:2; 27:16, 18

Deu   2:30; 34:9

Jos   2:11; 5:1

Jdg   3:10; 6:34; 8:3; 9:23; 11:29; 13:25; 14:6, 19; 15:14, 19

1 Sa   1:15; 10:6, 10; 11:6; 16:13-16, 23; 18:10; 19:9, 20, 23; 30:12

2 Sa   22:11, 16; 23:2

1 Ki   10:5; 18:12, 45; 19:11; 21:5; 22:21-24

2 Ki   2:9, 15, 16; 3:17; 19:7

1 Ch   5:26; 9:24; 12:18; 28:12

2 Ch   9:4; 15:1; 18:20-23; 20:14; 21:16; 24:20; 36:22

Ezr   1:1, 5

Neh   9:20, 30

Job   1:19; 4:9, 15; 6:4, 26; 7:7, 11; 8:2; 9:18; 10:12; 12:10; 15:2, 13, 30; 16:3; 17:1; 19:17; 20:3; 21:4, 18; 26:13; 27:3; 28:25; 30:15, 22; 32:8, 18; 33:4; 34:14; 37:21; 41:8

Psa   1:4; 11:6; 18:11, 16, 43; 31:6; 32:2; 33:6; 34:19; 35:5; 48:8; 51:12-14, 19; 55:9; 76:13; 77:4, 7; 78:8, 39; 83:14; 103:16; 104:3, 4, 29, 30; 106:33; 107:25; 135:7, 17; 139:7; 142:4; 143:4, 7, 10; 146:4; 147:18; 148:8

Pro   1:23; 11:13, 29; 14:29; 15:4, 13; 16:2, 18, 19, 32; 17:22, 27; 18:14; 25:14, 23, 28; 27:16; 29:11, 23; 30:4;

Ecc   1:6, 14, 17; 2:11, 17, 26; 3:19, 21; 4:4, 6, 16; 5:15; 6:9; 7:8, 9; 8:8; 10:4; 11:4, 5; 12:7

Isa   4:4; 7:2; 11:2, 4, 15; 17:13; 19:3, 14; 25:4; 26:9, 18; 27:8; 28:6; 29:10, 24; 30:1, 28; 31:3; 32:2, 15; 33:11; 34:16; 37:7; 38:16; 40:7, 13; 41:16, 29; 42:1, 5; 44:3; 48:16; 54:6; 57:13, 15, 16; 59:19, 21; 61:1, 3; 63:10, 11, 14; 64:5; 65:14; 66:2

Jer   2:24; 4:11, 12; 5:13; 10:13, 14; 13:24; 14:6; 18:17; 22:22; 49:32, 36; 51:1, 11, 16, 17; 52:23

Lam   4:20

Eze	1:4, 12, 20, 21; 2:2; 3:12, 14, 24; 5:2, 10, 12; 8:3; 10:17; 11:1, 5, 19, 24; 12:14; 13:3, 11, 13; 17:10, 21; 18:31; 19:12; 20:32; 21:12; 27:26; 36:26, 27; 37:1, 5, 6, 8-10, 14; 39:29; 42:16-20; 43:5
Dan	2:1, 3; 8:8; 11:4
Hos	4:12, 19; 5:4; 8:7; 9:7; 12:2; 13:15
Joel	3:1, 2
Amos	4:13
Jona	1:4; 4:8
Mic	2:7, 11; 3:8
Hab	1:11; 2:19
Hag	1:14; 2:5
Zec	2:10; 4:6; 5:9; 6:5, 8; 7:12; 12:1, 10; 13:2
Mal	2:15, 16

4.3 *Leb* (לֵב) in the Hebrew Bible (References)

Gen   6:5, 6; 8:21; 17:17; 18:5; 24:45; 27:41; 31:20; 34:3; 42:28; 45:26; 50:21

Exo   4:14, 21; 7:3, 13, 14, 22, 23; 8:11, 15, 28; 9:7, 12, 14, 21, 34, 35; 10:1, 20, 27; 11:10; 14:4, 8, 17; 15:8; 25:2; 28:3, 29, 30; 31:6; 35:5, 10, 21, 22, 25, 26, 29, 34, 35; 36:1, 2, 8

Num   16:28; 24:13; 32:7, 9

Deu   4:11; 28:65; 29:3, 18

Jos   1:20; 14:8

Jdg   5:9, 15, 16; 9:3; 16:15, 17, 18, 25; 18:20; 19:3, 5, 6, 22

Ruth 2:13; 3:7

1 Sa 1:13; 2:1; 4:13, 20; 6:6; 9:20; 10:9, 26; 17:32; 24:6; 25:25, 31, 36, 37; 27:1; 28:5

2 Sa 6:16; 7:21, 27; 13:20, 28, 33; 14:1; 15:6, 13; 17:10; 18:3, 14; 19:8, 20; 24:10

1 Ki 3:9, 12; 5:9; 8:23, 47, 66; 9:3; 10:24; 11:3; 12:26, 27, 33; 18:37; 21:7

2 Ki 5:26; 6:11; 9:24; 12:5; 14:10; 23:3

1 Ch 12:33, 38; 15:29; 16:10; 17:19; 28:9; 29:9

2 Ch 6:14, 38; 7:10, 11, 16; 9:23; 12:14; 17:6; 24:4; 25:19; 26:16; 29:31; 30:12, 22; 32:25, 26

Ezr   6:22; 7:27

Neh   2:2, 12; 3:38; 5:7; 6:8; 7:5

Est   1:10; 5:9; 6:6; 7:5

Job   1:8; 2:3; 7:17; 8:10; 11:13; 12:24; 15:12; 17:4; 23:16; 29:13; 31:7, 9, 27; 33:3; 34:14; 36:5,13; 37:1, 24; 41:16

Psa   4:8; 7:11; 9:2; 10:6, 11, 13, 17; 11:2; 12:3; 13:6; 14:1; 16:9; 17:3; 19:9, 15; 21:3; 22:15; 26:2; 27:3, 8, 14; 28:7; 31:13; 32:11; 33:11, 15, 21; 34:19; 35:25; 36:2, 11; 37:4, 15, 31; 38:9, 11; 39:4; 40:11, 13; 41:7; 44:19, 22; 45:2, 6; 46:3; 48:14; 49:4; 51:12, 19; 53:2; 55:5, 22; 57:8; 58:3; 61:3; 62:11; 64:7, 11; 66:18; 69:21; 74:8; 76:6; 78:8, 37; 81:13; 83:6; 84:3; 94:15; 97:11; 102:5; 105:3, 25; 107:12; 108:2; 109:22; 112:7, 8; 119:2, 10, 11, 32, 34, 36, 58, 69, 70, 80, 111, 112, 145, 161; 131:1; 138:1; 140:3; 141:4; 143:4; 147:3

Pro   2:2, 10; 3:1, 3, 5; 4:4, 23; 5:12; 6:14, 18, 21, 32; 7:3, 7, 10, 25; 8:5; 9:4, 16; 10:8, 13, 20, 21; 11:12, 20, 29; 12:8, 11, 20, 23, 25; 13:12; 14:10, 13, 14, 30, 33; 15:7,13-15, 21, 28, 30, 32; 16:1, 5, 9, 21, 23; 17:16, 18, 20, 22; 18:2, 12, 15; 19:3, 8, 21; 20:5, 9; 21:1, 4; 22:11, 15, 17; 23:7,

	12, 15, 17, 19, 26, 33, 34; 24:2, 17, 30, 32; 25:3, 20; 26:23, 25; 27:9, 11, 19, 23; 28:14, 26; 30:19; 31:11
Ecc	1:13, 16, 17; 2:1, 3, 10, 15, 20, 22, 23; 3:11, 17, 18; 5:1, 19; 7:2 4, 7, 21, 22, 25, 26; 8:5, 9, 11, 16; 9:1, 3, 7; 10:2, 3; 11:9, 10
Son	3:11; 5:2; 8:6
Isa	6:10; 15:5; 24:7; 29:13; 32:6; 33:18; 35:4; 38:3; 40:2; 41:22; 42:25; 44:19, 20; 46:8,12; 47:7, 10; 51:7; 57:1, 11, 15, 17; 59:13; 61:1; 63:4, 17; 65:14, 17; 66:14
Jer	3:10, 15-17; 4:9, 14, 18, 19; 5:21, 23; 7:24, 31; 8:18; 9:13, 25; 11:8, 20; 12:3, 11; 13:10; 14:14; 16:12; 17:1, 5, 9, 10; 18:12; 19:5; 20:9, 12; 22:17; 23:9, 16, 17, 20, 26; 24:7; 30:21, 24; 31:21, 33; 32:35, 39, 41; 44:21; 48:29, 36, 41; 49:16, 22; 51:1
Lam	1:20, 22; 2:18, 19; 3:21, 33, 65; 5:15, 17
Eze	2:4; 3:7; 6:9; 11:19, 21; 13:2, 17, 22; 14:3-5, 7; 18:31; 20:16; 21:12, 20; 22:14; 27:4, 25-27; 28:2, 6, 8, 17; 32:9; 33:31; 36:26; 40:4; 44:5, 7, 9
Dan	1:8; 10:12
Hos	2:16; 4:11; 7:6, 11, 14; 10:2; 11:8; 13:6, 8
Amos	2:16
Oba	1:3
Nah	2:11
Zep	3:14
Zec	7:12; 10:7; 12:5
Mal	2:2; 3:24

4.4 Proverbs 20:27

Proverbs 20:27 is an excellent example for demonstrating how necessary it is to do linguistic anthropological research. The English versions show significant enough variants to arouse more curiosity. Especially NIV is quite different from both NRSV and NKJV, and TEV is different from all three of them. The problem of translation is even more complex in the Bemba version (**BAIBELE** 1956 – Bemba is a Bantu language widely spoken in Zambia) as it leans heavily on the English text. The Nyanja text (another major Bantu language in Zambia), however, appears to be more considerate of the original Hebrew text than its Bemba counterpart.

NEW INTERNATIONAL VERSION *NIV*

[27] The lamp of the LORD searches the spirit of a man; it searches out his inmost being.

NEW REVISED STANDARD VERSION *NRSV*

[27] The human spirit is the lamp of the LORD, searching every inmost part.

TODAY'S ENGLISH VERSION *TEV*

[27] The LORD gave us mind and conscience; we cannot hide from ourselves.

NEW KING JAMES VERSION *NKJV*

[27] The spirit of a man is the lamp of the Lord, searching all the inner depths of his heart.

BAIBELE [BEMBA 1956]

Kampingu wa muntunse ni nyali yakwa Yehoba, iifwayafwaya monse mu ncende sha mu nda.

The inner judge [conscience] of mortal man is the lamp of Jehovah, it searches all the places of the innermost).

BUKU LOYERA [NYANJA 1998]

Mpweya wa munthu uli ngati nyale ya Chauta; nyaleyo imafufuza ziwalo zonse zam'kati.

The breath of a person is like the lamp of Chauta [= YHWH]; that lamp searches out/investigates all of [his/her] inner members/body parts.

Some questions:

1. Is the empahsis on man [his 'spirit', his 'conscience'], or is it on God [his lamp]?

2. In the absence of the Hebrew *nefesh* and *ruach*, on what basis is the English term 'spirit' justified?

3. Where English versions either use spirit or mind and conscience, the Hebrew text has *nesama*. What does *nesama* mean, and do other contexts in which *nesama* appears justify a rendering that reads 'spirit' or mind and conscience?

4. The second line of the verse makes specific reference to the body, in particular to the rounded inner part of the belly (the Hebrew uses an architectural word). What is the relationship between *nesama* and the places of the innermost – the rounded inner part – of the belly?

Some observations on the form:

1. The meaning of the Hebrew word *nesama* (a noun, sing. fem.) is first and foremost breath.[10] Living creatures are categorized in Hebrew thought as "breath-beings" (Wolff 1984:97).

2. To render *nesama* of *adam* in v27 (נִשְׁמַת אָדָם) as spirit or mind and conscience lacks strength in the light of all other contexts in which the word is used. Nowhere else does *nesama* contain the meaning of spirit or mind and conscience.

3. It could be better to stick to the overwhelming meaning of *nesama* as breath, since the **anthropological language** of the second line (the places of the innermost) is more naturally continued.

4. Bearing in mind that *nesama* means the breath of man, and by extension his very life, the Bemba term *kampingu* is no match for *nesama*. *Kampingu* is a term that is clearly associated with the *SEIC* of a person, whereas *nesama* strictly maintains a physiological meaning.

5. Considering the difficult Hebrew text and putting emphasis on *nesama* with its prime meaning of breath, Wolff is of the opinion that this would justify a shift from *ner* [lamp] to *noser* [to guard or protect].

A suggestion:

Taking into account the findings, an alternative translation could be:

> *It is Yahweh who 'guards' the breath of man.*
> *He searches all the places of the innermost*

A possible Bemba translation could read as follows:

> *Uwacingilila umupu [or umweo] wa muntu ni Yawe,*
> *ewafwayafwaya monse mu ncende sha mu nda.*

> The breath (or 'life-force') of a person – Yahweh guards it;
> he searches all the places of the innermost.

---

[10] *Nesama* occurs in the OT 24 times. The characteristic of a living person is his *nesama*, that is to say, that he has breath (Job 27:3; Jos 11:11; 1 Ki 17:17 etc.) (Wolff 1984:97).

I would not want to completely exclude the possibility of a figurative usage of *nesama*, though personally I would like to maintain the alternative reading as presented above.[11]

Wendland comments:

> The term "breath" here could well refer to man's "life-force", breathed into humans at the time of creation (Gen. 2:7). It is not only physical "life" that is given here, but also potential moral, intellectual, and spiritual capabilities. There does seem to be an allusion here to the original creation event. Man's life-force is a testifying trace of the divine in fallen mankind. Like a shining lamp it bears witness to the holy Creator and man's moral responsibility before the LORD (even though in his fallen state man no longer recognizes this aspect of "the natural knowledge of God" within his being). Perhaps in a figurative way, this "breath" is analogous to the human conscience. In any case, people cannot hide their deepest thoughts, plans, purposes, and motives – whether good or evil – from their Creator. Having said that, of course we must add that the meaning of a proverb is always contextualized by the setting in which it is used and the current discourse in which it is applied.[12]

---

[11] See Badenberg, 2003.

[12] Dr. Ernst Wendland, longtime UBS Bible Consultant, Lusaka, Zambia. Personal correspondence 7 June, 2003.

4.5   Corinthian Issues[13]

Bible translation has been going on in the Bemba language for many years. Several different editions have been produced over time. The first complete translation of the Bible was published in 1956. It was called **BAIBELE**. Since then various attempts have been made to revise this early work. In 1973 a more contemporary version of the New Testament *(Icipangano Cipya)* saw completion. Eight years later, in 1981, the *Bible wa Mushilo* appeared and targeted Roman Catholic readers. But this translation soon fell into dislike, mainly because of its orthography, as people found it very difficult to read. That is why the Bible Society of Zambia decided in 1993 to start a new translation project of the whole Bible. Translation of the New Testament, now called *Ishiwi lyakwa Lesa – Icipangano Cipya,* was completed in 2001 but publication was delayed for another two years.

The study of the terms body, soul, and spirit in the popular *New International Version* (NIV) of the Bible indicates that the usage of these terms does not convey a consistent meaning.[14]

The situation in the Bemba New Testament[15] *(Icipangano Cipya)* is even more complex, if not to say bewildering. The English word spirit (which itself is the rendering of the two Greek terms *pneuma*[16] and *psyche*[17]) is conveyed by *four* different Bemba words:[18] *mutima,*[19] *mweo,*[20] *mano,*[21] and *mupashi.*[22] A similar situation applies concerning the English term soul (which itself is the rendering

---

[13] The following material is taken from an earlier work. See Badenberg 1999/2002: Chap. 6.

[14] In Matthew 5:3 the Greek term *pneuma* is rendered spirit. The same term is translated soul in Luke 10:27. But in Luke 2:35 soul is the translation of *psyche*. The situation is even more complex in Bemba. Matthew 5:3 in Bemba uses the term *mutima* for the English term spirit and the Greek term *pneuma*. In Luke 10:27 is the Bemba term *mweo* used to translate the English term soul and the Greek term *psyche*. And in Luke 2:35 the term *mutima* is used to convey the English term soul and the Greek term *psyche*. For more references see Appendix 8.

[15] The Bemba New Testament *(Icipangano Cipya)*, United Bible Societies, 1973.

[16] Mt 5:3; 26:41; Lk 1:47; Jn 11:33; 1Cor 4:21; 1Thess 5:23 etc.

[17] Lk 1:47; 1:80.

[18] All words have dropped the initial vowel of the prefix.

[19] With the working definition "psyche" for *mutima* compare Mt 5:3; 26:41; Mk 2:8; Jn 11:33; 13:21; Rom 8:16; 1Cor 4:21; 7:34; 16:18; 2Cor 4:13; Gal 6:18; Phil 1:27; 1Pet 3:4.

[20] With the working definition "life-force" for *mweo* compare: Mt 27:50; Lk 8:55; 23:46; Jn 19:30; Acts 7:59; Jam 2:26.

[21] *Mano* means wisdom, intelligence. With this definition compare Lk 1:17.80; 1Thess 5:23.

[22] Cited are Scriptures which do not refer to the Holy Spirit. Acts 23:9; 1Cor 2:11; 5:3.4.5; 6:17; 14:14.15.16; 2Cor 7:1; 11:4; Col 2:5; 2Tim 4:22; Heb 4:12; 1Jn 4:1 (*mipashi* plural of *mupashi*).

of the two Greek terms *pneuma*[23] and *psyche*[24]) which translates two Bemba words: *mweo*[25] and *mutima*.[26]

The difficulties that arise lie in determining the precise meaning each time *spirit* or *soul* is to be translated. For example, John 13:21 says that Jesus "was troubled in spirit". The statement clearly indicates that Jesus underwent a change in his psychic disposition as he was faced with the presence of his betrayer. Spirit in this context refers to his psyche (*SEIC*) rather than the being that continues his personality after death. The Bemba term *mutima*,[27] as used in the Bemba New Testament, does, in this instance, convey this very same notion.

1 Cor 5:3

The situation gets extremely complicated, for example, in 1 Cor 5:3. Paul is greatly agitated over the reported sexual immorality among the Christians of the Corinthian church. He points out that this situation is deeply affecting him. Moreover, the lenient attitude of the church in taking appropriate action causes him much grief. His physical absence makes no difference at all in the way he feels. Since he is with them "in spirit", he has the same feelings and judgment regarding the case as if he were present in person. His feelings and his thoughts are completely dominated by the unacceptable behaviour of the perpetrator.

The Bemba translation speaks of Paul being together with them *mu mupashi*[28] (in spirit). It was shown earlier that *umupashi* is first of all a spirit being with a *SEIC* and personality of its own. It is the spirit double of a person and also the being that survives the death of the body as well as the being that retains and continues the personality of a person in the afterlife. The range of meanings that can be ascribed to *umupashi* would hardly express what the English idiom "to be with you in spirit" conveys in the context of Paul's statement.

Even if a translation of *"mu mupashi"* is possible, would Bemba-speaking people really grasp the intellectual and emotional dimension of an English idiom? Would *"mu mupashi"* to them not tend to convey the personality of a spirit being? Could we possibly say that Paul was with them through his spirit double? Not really! It is clear that Paul, his *SEIC*, was deeply moved and that his feelings, thoughts, and intentions were directed toward the events at the Corinthian Church.

---

[23] Lk 10:27.

[24] Mt 10:28; Lk 1:46; Heb 6:19 etc. .

[25] Compare Mt 10:28; 16:26; 22:37; Lk 10:27; Mk 8:36.37; 12:30; Heb 4:12.

[26] Compare Mt 26:38; Mk 14:34; Lk 1:46; 2:35; 1Thess 5:23; Heb 6:19, 1Pt 2:11.

[27] Jn 13:21 reads in Bemba *(Icipangano Cipya)*: *Ilyo Yesu asosele ifi, no mutima wakwe wasakamikwa,..."* lit., "when Jesus said these things, his psyche was caused to be worried, to be anxious."

[28] Bemba translation *(Icipangano Cipya)* of 1Cor 5:3: *...lelo mu mupashi mwena tuli pamo bonse*, lit., "but in *mupashi*, however, we are all together." *(Ishiwi lyakwa Lesa Icipangano Cipya 2003)*: *Ine nangu ndi ukutali, mu mupashi mwena tuli na imwe pamo.*

The context suggests that Paul has the Corinthian Church **on his mind**, that the Christians there are object of his **thinking, contemplation**, and surely, of his **prayers**. Translating a text should not only be correct in the sense of linguistic correspondence, but it ought to first and foremost capture its message, so as to enable readers to gain the proper meaning for themselves.

1 Cor 5:5

1 Cor 5:5 does pose another challenge. Paul is instructing the church on the kind of action they are to take. In the final analysis, he says, it would be far better for the perpetrator to suffer loss during his earthly days than to suffer loss on the day of the Lord ("...and his spirit saved on the day of the Lord"). Paul's concern is for the future condition of the person with respect to Jesus' coming.

Putting the English term spirit put in the context of the Lord's Day suggests that Paul includes a dimension of the person's life which goes beyond the death of his body! The focus of attention is that even death is not able to extinguish the man's individual personality. Viewed from this angle, the Bemba word *umu-pashi*[29] transfers a powerful message to its listeners.

The problem Bemba listeners might have is that within the short context of three verses (1 Cor 5:3-5) two different concepts are expressed yet translated with one and the same Bemba word. The whole of 1 Corinthians is actually rather ambiguous on the usage of terms.[30] Paul speaks of praying with his spirit[31] *(mu mupashi wandi)*; at the same time he prays with his mind *(mu mano)*. He also sings with both with his spirit *(mu mupashi wandi)* and with his mind *(mu mano mwine)*. Bemba thinking hardly distinguishes between intellectual processes which occur in the mind or in the spirit.

One area where confusion of concepts may have a serious implication is evangelism. There is hardly time to go into depth and explain how things relate to one another during public evangelistic meetings as is the case during seminars and teaching sessions. This could create substantial disadvantages in proclaiming the message to the listeners, since one cannot address issues in the "proper" way. How shall listeners hear "properly" if the talking is not done "properly"?

The quality of a translation of the Bible should be measured in terms of two aspects: it should neither neglect nor corrupt indigenous speakers' ideas concerning these concepts nor should it empty Scripture of its content.[32]

---

[29] Bemba translation *(Icipangano Cipya)* of 1Cor 5:5 *...ukuti umupashi wakwe wena uka-pusuke pa bushiku bwa Mfumu*, lit., "so that his *umupashi*, however, will be saved on the day of the King [Lord]."

[30] Compare 1Cor 2:11; 5:4; 6:17; 14:14.15.16.32 (plural). Also 2Cor 7:1.

[31] 1Cor 14:15. I am of the opinion that in this verse, Paul does not refer to the Holy Spirit.

[32] A fine exposition on contextualizing key terms on principalities and powers is found in Pattemore (1994a:116-129) and Pattemore (1994b:315-321).

Bemba Anthropology and some Implications concerning the Person of the Holy Spirit

Some aspects of the Bemba concept of *umupashi* overlap with those which are found in the Bible with reference to the Holy Spirit. But others are significantly different from biblical thought. Here are some aspects which overlap:

First, *umupashi* is neither male nor female. Spirit beings have no difference of gender but are complete; they are of twin-gender.[33] The gender of *umupashi* is of no significance at all. This is demonstrated by the fact that Bemba boys and girls can receive and bear the same names! This raises the issue of what personal pronoun to use for *umupashi*. The Greek word for spirit is neuter, but translations normally use the masculine pronoun. In German terms like *Wesen* (being) are also neuter and the neuter pronoun is used, without necessarily implying loss of personality – not to mention that *Mädchen* (young girl) is also neuter! English may be more problematic here (although sometimes a small child can be termed 'it' if in context the gender is not known and is not important). In what follows below *umupashi* is referred to as 'it'. However, this is not at all intended to imply absence of personality *(SEIC)*.

Second, *umupashi* is thought to live in the wind or air, is omnipresent, and keeps close to its human companion and the community at large. *Umupashi* is neither counted as part of the human body, nor does it have a body itself, because it is like air/wind. Yet, there exists the idea that *umupashi* is so closely attached to a human that one can speak of it indwelling the body or residing in the *SEIC* of a person.[34] *Umupashi* is not thought to possess body warmth on its own but is accredited with the capability of bringing down the body temperature of a person running a high fever *(mpepo)* if asked to do so.

Physiological factors such as hunger, thirst, tiredness, sleep, shedding of tears, laughing, pain, love, and fear, do not affect *umupashi* ontologically, though he might undergo *psychic* changes. For example, it can be angered, suffer frustration, experience happiness and gratitude by the actions (or behaviour in general) of its human companion. All psychic dispositions are temporal and affect *umupashi* in his *SEIC*.

A person cannot normally see his own *umupashi* but *umupashi* can show his presence in rare circumstances in dreams in the form of a white dove *(nkunda ya buuta)*, a white chicken *(inkoko ya buuta)*, or as a person dressed in bright, white

---

[33] "Transcendent beings …possess both the male and female mode of being human." Hinfelaar (1994:6).

[34] *Pantu ifyaba mu muntu fishibwa fye ku mupashi wakwe wine uwaba mu nda yakwe*, lit., "because what the things in a person are, they are just known to his *mupashi* himself, who is inside him, in his psyche."

cloth *(insalu ya buuta)*.[35] These figures, however, are simply different manifestations of *umupashi;* they are not an exact replica of its appearance.

The situation is different where *umupashi* of another person is concerned. Dreams, for example, featuring a person dressed in white cloth, might be identified as the *umupashi* of one's wife (or vice versa) as some features can be clearly identified. This observation does suggest that *umupashi* possesses physical features which are identical to those of its human companion. That is to say, *umupashi* is the genuine, perfect and superior spirit double of a person.

Third, *umupashi* is perceived as a good-natured, benevolent being. Its *SEIC* features only permanent positive character attributes and its dealings with a person are explicitly positive even if some kind of reprimand or "punishment" (like sickness), should be necessary.[36]

Umupashi of a person is thought to be very understanding and knowledgeable about the worries and problems which bother him or her. It can help troubled persons through dreams in order to make them rest assured of its presence, especially in times of sickness when the approach of death is feared.

The Scriptures make no reference to the Holy Spirit being of either gender. The Greek word for Spirit, *pneuma*, is neuter in gender,[37] but scripture references speak of the Spirit as a person with the personal pronoun "he".[38] The interest the Bible pursues in introducing us to the triune God seems to be in featuring the **personality** of the Holy Spirit rather than his gender. Thus, the Spirit has no regard for a person's gender in the distribution of spiritual gifts. He will give gifts as He deems right to each Christian, man or woman alike.[39]

Bemba Christians appear – on account of their anthropology – to have less difficulty in understanding the personality of the Holy Spirit than Christians from the Western world.[40] The fact that the Bible speaks of the Holy Spirit as having a

---

[35] The color white is of great importance to the Bemba symbol system.

[36] People who adhere to traditional views allege sickness to a wrong one committed against his *umupashi*. As a measure of education, *umupashi* withdraws his protection and a person is easy prey to forces of ill will. Only intercession will mend and revive damaged relations. The interceding person (probably a honorable family member) would say words like this: *BaChanda mubeleleko umuntu wenu uluse,* meaning: "*BaChanda* (forebear of whom the name was inherited) please forgive your person, that is, make him to recover again." Compare also Wendland, "Christology," 16.

[37] O'Donovan (1996:129).

[38] Jn 16:13 "When the Holy Spirit of truth comes, he will guide you into all truth."

[39] Compare 1Cor 12:11; 1Pet 4:10.

[40] From 1991 to 1993 I was Pastor of a Church in a small mining town in Zambia. At one time I preached a series of sermons on the Holy Spirit trying to emphasize that the Holy Spirit is a person, rather than some kind of influence or a type of power. I would have been much better advised to apply elements of their own concept, if only I had then known how to go about it more constructively.

mind and a will[41] as well as emotions,[42] is another advantage on the side of Bemba people in grasping more easily the personhood of the Holy Spirit.

The idea that dreams might have significant messages is biblically underscored by the accounts of Jacob's, Joseph's, and Daniel's dreams, to mention but a few examples. Western man – and missionary personnel alike – are not always receptive to the idea that dreams are a valid communication between God and his people.[43]

A further overlapping feature of *umupashi* and the Holy Spirit is that both share a *SEIC* of positive nature. Their dealings with people are characterized by seeking the best for them. The statement in John 16:17, where Jesus promises his disciples the coming and perpetual presence of the Holy Spirit as the Counsellor,[44] is a powerful and easily grasped truth among Bemba Christians.

The stumbling block which Bemba Christians must be aware of concerns the fact that a person might be able to permanently change – and even ruin – the *SEIC* of his *umupashi*. This can happen when a person pursues a lifestyle that is against the appropriate code of behaviour which will eventually turn the benevolent companion into a malevolent double.

Consequently, the person concerned will equally suffer a change in his own *SEIC*. Moreover the *SEIC* of his spirit double transforms itself into a malevolent spirit double (*icibanda*). Such a person has forfeited his potential of becoming a *Mupashi Mukankala*, a generous, important spirit forebear (Hinfelaar 1994). His name, his *imibele* (individual personality), will never again appear in the family lineage due to a ruined *SEIC*.

Christians are, however, under no circumstances in a position to change or even ruin the *SEIC* of the Holy Spirit. Behaviour that is not pleasing to Him and sin committed against God and/or fellow believers, does not bring about the transformation of the Spirit's *SEIC* as the Counsellor into an enemy par excellence.

The danger of simple and comparative analogy is real and contains syncretistic potential. A loose and carelessly applied analogy of *umupashi* and the Holy Spirit may bring confusion and generate misunderstandings. The biblical texts know nothing about the Spirit's likeness in form to individual physical features which He would share with individual believers. The communication of the Gospel message, of which the Holy Spirit is an essential part, ought to happen in

> ... linguistic terms that people can immediately grasp and in cognitive categories which their ethnic background has already in certain respects prepared them to receive ... .[45]

---

[41] Compare Acts 16:7.

[42] Compare Rom 14:17; 15:30; Eph 4:30.

[43] See also Steyne (1996:124-126). Willoughby comments: "...but it cannot be disputed that the Israelites recognized dreams as a mode of communicating the divine will" (1970:91).

[44] The Greek term *parakletos* also means: an intercessor, consoler, advocate, comforter.

[45] Wendland (1991:15-16).

This calls for serious investigation and necessary expertise.

Just to pursue this point a little further, a question could be raised as to whether the Holy Spirit is in essence conceived as the spirit double of God. In Bemba the Holy Spirit is translated as *Mupashi Wamushilo* (Spirit of taboo, that on which a prohibition was imposed, by extension then Spirit of Holiness) or *Mupashi wakwa Lesa* (*Mupashi* of God).

This issue must remain an unfinished one as it would go beyond the scope and intentions of this handbook. I have merely attempted to point out a topic for further research.

Closing Remarks

The essential feature of this handbook is the multitude of questions which it poses. A second feature is no doubt the very noticeable absence of the corresponding answers. The arrangement of these two features has produced one of the unique aspects of this book. The other unique aspect consists surely in the fact that it is up to the readers to discover the appropriate answers for themselves.

Based on the targeted theme as set out, these questions have covered the five areas which are essential for research into the concept of man – *notions of the body,* the *Seat of the Emotions*, *Intellect*, *Character* or *personality traits [SEIC]* and *notions concerning the existence of a person after the death of the body*. However, it is all too apparent that not all questions relevant to these five areas could be taken into account, for the simple reason that the manifold variety of human societies in this world is far too complex.

Nevertheless I hope that through the content of these topics which I have described I have succeeded in awakening in many readers enough enthusiasm to set about their own investigations. The questions which are missing in this handbook, or yet more detailed ones, would then emerge of themselves for interested researchers. I would even venture to suggest that anyone who has once begun to dip a finger into other cultures will indeed not be able to withdraw it.

At this point I may be permitted to emphasise once more that this *handbook*, forms a combined package with the *textbook* on animism by Lothar Käser, providing a so far unique method of research into the concept of man among other cultures.

I therefore hope that as many keen researchers as possible will travel to these unfamiliar cultural worlds to undertake investigations. Not that this task is at all easy, even with this package. As well as a lot of patience it requires a certain degree of obstinacy to 'keep at it'. However, one thing is sure: there is a lot to discover for those who are not afraid of work – and of frequent frustration. The reward for all the effort is indeed overwhelming!

A key dimension of the reward is the acquired knowledge, creating whole new opportunities of communication with the members of the host culture.

'Keep asking questions': this is of course true in a general sense because communication is the main task of people living and working in an intercultural environment. But it is also true in special measure for missionary personnel whose chief concern is the communication of God.

'Keep asking questions': Hendrik Kraemer perceived the vital contribution of this discipline already six decades ago, when the value of anthropology for Christian mission was only visible on the distant horizon. For him the benefits of careful study of other cultures fulfilled a purpose: *"for the sake of doing the missionary task well and making the Christian approach an intelligent, constructive one"* (1947:341).

It is in this sense that I wish this book and its readers every success!

Appendix 1
Bemba Terminology Relating to the 'Soul'

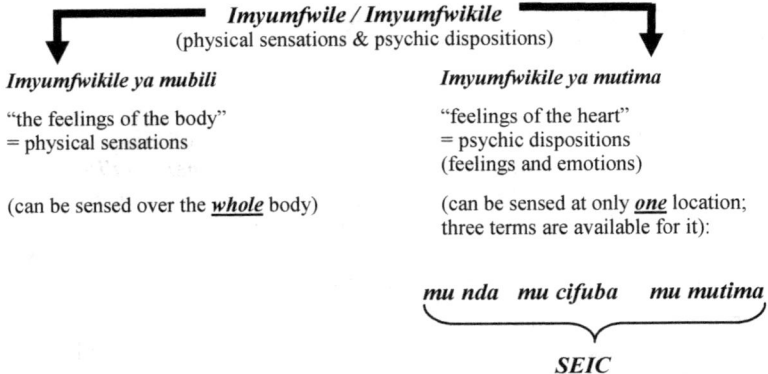

Imyumfwile / Imyumfwikile
(physical sensations & psychic dispositions)

Imyumfwikile ya mubili

"the feelings of the body"
= physical sensations

(can be sensed over the ***whole*** body)

Imyumfwikile ya mutima

"feelings of the heart"
= psychic dispositions
(feelings and emotions)

(can be sensed at only ***one*** location;
three terms are available for it):

mu nda   mu cifuba   mu mutima

SEIC

1. These three terms describe the psyche as the seat of the emotions, the intellect and character *(SEIC)*.
2. All three terms have the same basic meaning, but are not always interchangeable.
3. Each one emphasises particular aspects of the *SEIC*.

mu nda ("inside, in the abdominal cavity, the innermost area")

- not an organ; indicates the whole inner abdominal cavity, including the stomach and intestines e.g. *casungulula mabu mu nda* (lit.: that made my liver melt right inside)
- as a euphemism for the female lower abdomen

mu cifuba ("in the chest cavity")

- aspect of the physicality of the *SEIC*
- not used extensively in the language

mu mutima ("inside the heart")

- aspect of the *SEIC* in relation to a person's qualities of character or features of personality

(***mu-*** a prefix with a variety of applications. It characterises objects such that they appear as locations in space and time).

Appendix 2
Chuuk Terminology Relating to the 'Soul'

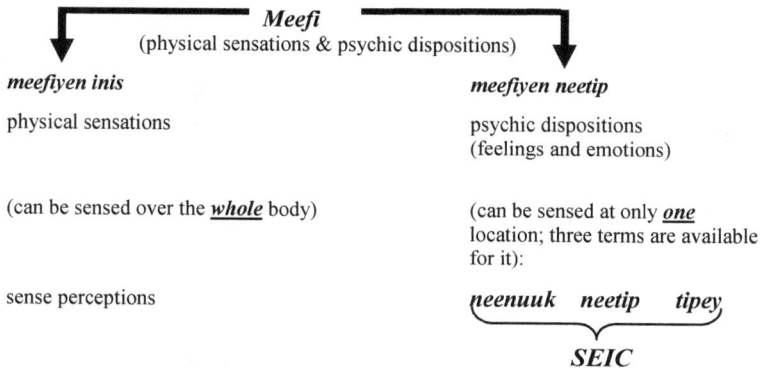

Meefi
(physical sensations & psychic dispositions)

meefiyen inis

physical sensations

(can be sensed over the **whole** body)

sense perceptions

meefiyen neetip

psychic dispositions
(feelings and emotions)

(can be sensed at only **one**
location; three terms are available
for it):

neenuuk   neetip   tipey

SEIC

1. These three terms describe the psyche as the seat of the emotions, intellect and character *(SEIC)*.
2. They are in most instances mutually interchangeable.
3. Each one highlights particular aspects of the *SEIC*.

neenuuk (located in the upper abdominal cavity, "in the middle")

- aspect of the physical affinity of the *SEIC*

neetip ("location of the physical disposition")

- seat of all intellectual processes
  (e.g. intentions, willpower, decision-making etc.)
- a euphemism for the sexual organs
- in particular a euphemism for the uterus and the female sexual organs

tipey

- aspect of the *SEIC* in relation to a person's qualities of character or personality traits

(*nee-* a prefix with a variety of applications. It characterises objects such that they appear as locations in space and time)

Appendix 3
Linguistic Notes in Bemba, English and Hebrew

Bemba	English	Hebrew
Umubili	**Body**	**Basar**
• body parts • body functions • body feelings	• body parts • body functions • body feelings	• flesh/ body • relationship • weakness
Umutima	**Soul**	**Nefesh**
• seat of the emotions *(Imyumfwikile ya mutima)* • intellectual processes: (thinking, remembering, reflecting, planning, pondering etc.) • personality traits / qualities of character *(Imibele)*	• psyche • emotions • whole person ("the poor soul") • "being which survives the death of the body" • embodiment of a particular quality: (e.g. 'he is the soul of discretion = he can be trusted to keep a secret')	• throat, gullet, pharynx • desire • breathing • soul, better *SEIC* • (seat of numerous emotions) • neck • life • person • personal pronoun 'I'
Umupashi	*spirit*	**Ruach**

• Being which perpetuates one's personality after the death of the body
• 'spirit double' of a living person:
  - but possesses its own *SEIC*, hence its own personality (albeit *only* positive qualities of character)
  - equates to the person
  - *sometimes reveals negative emotions*
• being which forms and develops the features of one's personality (one's *SEIC*)
	• character/ features of a group/ institution: (e.g. a different spirit is ruling here)
	• mood: (e.g. 'he is in high spirits')
	• true essence of a quality or activity: (e.g. 'a remark made in the spirit of friendliness')
	• synonym for 'soul'
	• 'spirit being' (negative overtones)
		• wind
		• breath
		• life-force
		• mind
		• disposition
		• willpower
		
		Leb
		• heart
		• feeling/ instinct
		• wish/ desire
		• reason/ good sense
		• resolve

Bibliography

Ablaßmeier, Reinhard. 1992. "Susto – eine psychosomatische Erkrankung? Ansichten der *quedada*, einer Erkrankung des 'Susto-Komplexes', mit der psychosomatischen Brille." In *Ritual und Heilung: Eine Einführung in die Medizinethnologie.* Katarina Greifeld (Hg.). 2003. 3. grundlegend überarbeitete und erweiterte Auflage. Berlin: Dietrich Reimer Verlag.

Badenberg, Robert. 2002. 2nd ed. *The Body, Soul and Spirit Concept of the Bemba: Fundamental Characteristics of Being Human of an African Ethnic Group.* Edition iwg, mission academics scripts vol. 9. Bonn: Verlag für Kultur und Wissenschaft.

Badenberg, Robert. 2003. "'Barbarische' Zustände in der Mission?" In *Mission in fremden Kulturen: Beiträge zur Missionsethnologie.* Festschrift für Lothar Käser zu seinem 65. Geburtstag. Edition afem, mission academics vol. 15. Nürnberg: Verlag für Theologie und Religionswissenschaft.

Badenberg, Robert. 2008. 2nd ed. *Sickness and Healing: A Case Study on the Dialectic of Culture and Personality.* Edition afem, mission academics vol. 11. Nürnberg: VTR Publications.

Baker, Larry N. 2003. "A Semantic Study of 'Soul' in the Hebrew Old Testament." Paper presented at the Evangelical Theological Society – SW Region, March 22.

Barthel, Thomas S. 1964. "Ethnolinguistische Polynesienforschung." In *Animism: Einführung in seine begrifflichen Grundlagen.* Lothar Käser. 2004. Bad Liebenzell: Verlag der Liebenzeller Mission.

Greifeld, Katarina und Bettina Schmidt. 2003. "Medizinische Systeme Süd- und Afroamerikas." In *Ritual und Heilung: Eine Einführung in die Medizinethnologie.* Katarina Greifeld (Hg.). 2003. 3. grundlegend überarbeitete und erweiterte Auflage. Berlin: Dietrich Reimer Verlag.

Hinfelaar, Hugo F. 1994. *Bemba Speaking Women of Zambia in a Century of Religious Change (1892-1992).* Studies of Religion in Africa, eds., Adrian Hastings and Marc R. Spencer. Leiden: E. J. Brill.

Käser, Lothar. 1977. "Der Begriff Seele bei den Insulanern von Truk." Unpublished Ph.D. Dissertation, Albert-Ludwigs-Universität Freiburg i. Br.

Käser, Lothar. 1989. *Die Besiedlung Mikronesiens: Eine Ethnologisch-Linguistische Untersuchung.* Berlin: Dietrich Reimer Verlag.

Käser, Lothar. 2014. *Foreign Cultures: An Introduction to Ethnology for Development Aid Workers and Church Workers Abroad.* Nürnberg: VTR Publications.

Käser, Lothar. 2014. *Animism – A Cognitive Approach: An Introduction to the Basic Notions Underlying the Concepts of the World and of Man Held by Ethnic Societies, for the Benefit of Those Working Overseas in Development Aid and in the Church.* Nürnberg: VTR Publications.

Knödler, Friedemann. 2006. *Die Beschneidung des Sundanesen: Eine Studie über die Inkulturierung der christlichen Kirche in Westjava.* Korntaler Reihe vol. 3. Nürnberg: Verlag für Theologie und Religionswissenschaft.

Kraemer, Hendrik. 1947. *The Christian Message in a Non-Christian World.* London: Edinburgh House Press.

Kutalek, Ruth. 2003. "Medizinische Systeme in Afrika." In *Ritual und Heilung: Eine Einführung in die Medizinethnologie.* Katarina Greifeld (Hg.). 2003. 3. grundlegend überarbeitete und erweiterte Auflage. Berlin: Dietrich Reimer Verlag.

Lee, Dorothy. 1959. *Freedom and Culture.* Harvard University: Prentice Hall, Inc.

Lomen, Martin. 2003. *Sünde und Scham im biblischen und islamischen Kontext: Ein ethno-hermeneutischer Beitrag zum christlich-islamischen Dialog.* Edition afem, mission scripts vol. 21. Nürnberg: Verlag für Theologie und Religionswissenschaft.

Nunn, H.P.V. 1973. 5th ed. *A Short Syntax of New Testament Greek.* London: Cambridge University Press.

O'Donovan, Wilbur, Jr. 1996. 2nd ed. *Biblical Christianity in African Perspective.* Carlisle: The Paternoster Press.

Olson, Bruce. 1978. 2nd printing. *Bruchko.* Carol Stream: Creation House.

Pattemore, Stephen W. 1994a. "Principalities and Powers in Urak Lawoi'. Introduction: Contextualizing Key Terms." *The Bible Translator* vol. 45, no. 1: 116-129.

Pattemore, Stephen W. 1994b. "Principalities and Powers in Urak Lawoi'. Contextualizing the Supernatural." *The Bible Translator* vol. 45, no. 3: 315-321.

Ritchie, Mark Andrew. 2000. 2nd ed. *Spirit of the Rainforest.* Chicago: Island Lake Press.

Steyne, Philip M. 1996. 4th Edition. *Gods of Power: A Study of the Beliefs and Practices of Animists.* Columbia, SC: Impact International Foundation.

The White Fathers Bemba-English Dictionary. 1991. Revised edition. Ndola, Zambia: The Society of the Missionaries for Africa.

Wendland, Ernst. 1991. "'Who do People say I am?' Contextualizing Christology in Africa." *AJET* vol. 10, no. 2: 13-32.

Wiher, Hannes. 2003. *Shame and Guilt: A Key to Cross-Cultural Ministry.* Edition iwg, mission academics scripts vol. 10. Bonn: Verlag für Kultur und Wissenschaft.

Willoughby, W. C. 1970 (reprint). *The Soul of the Bantu: A Sympathetic Study of the Magico-Religious Practices and Beliefs of the Bantu Tribes of Africa.* Garden City, NY: Doubleday, Doran & Company, Inc., Westport, CT: Negro Universities Press.

Wolff, Hans Walter. 1984. 4., durchges. Aufl. *Anthropologie des Alten Testaments.* Munich: Chr. Kaiser Verlag.

Foreign Cultures

by Lothar Käser

An Introduction to Ethnology
for Development Aid Workers and Church Workers Abroad

In recent decades foreign cultures have not just loomed large for Europeans seeking holiday destinations. Since the 1960s increasing numbers of professionals such as teachers, doctors, agronomists, and other professional workers and missionaries from Europe and America have been partnering local churches in Africa, Asia and Latin America whose fellowships are often very differently organised. When preparing these specialists, development agencies and missions often overlook the knowledge and insights that ethnology and cultural anthropology have to offer, help that makes it easier for professionals to take their bearings, to be well integrated, and to go about their work more effectively. This book deals with such issues.

For future theorists dealing with foreign cultures (ethnologists, anthropologists, etc.) there is now a whole range of brilliantly written textbooks. However, for development aid practitioners, whether secular workers or church workers, these introductory works are overloaded with theory and are thus difficult to digest. What has been missing until now is a simple introduction to the basic concepts which could enable a European working in foreign surroundings to come to terms with the ethnological literature relevant for his activities overseas, to recognise these essential concepts woven into the daily cultural reality of life and work, and to work with them and to bring to bear his or her own analysis. This book is a simplified introduction along these lines, not just written for the target readers just mentioned, but also for students of ethnology/cultural anthropology and for those who frequent ethnological museums.

The author is a professor of anthropology with relevant experience of the issues. He spent five years working in the South Pacific, and has visited Africa, Asia and South America on many occasions for research.

Pb. • pp. 290 • £ 22.50 • $ 37.50 • € 29.95
ISBN 978-3-95776-113-2

VTR Publications • Gogolstr. 33 • 90475 Nürnberg • Germany
info@vtr-online.com • http://www.vtr-online.com

Animism
A Cognitive Approach

An Introduction to the Basic Notions Underlying the Concepts of the World and of Man Held by Ethnic Societies, for the Benefit of Those Working Overseas in Development Aid and in the Church

by Lothar Käser

Textbook
to Robert Badenberg's Handbook
The Concept of Man in Non-Western Cultures

In European and other western societies animism is often equated with occultism, spiritism and even with satanism, is evaluated according to European and Christian criteria, and is consequently misunderstood. Such an approach, together with lack of knowledge of the conceptual foundations of animistic thought forms, proves to be a particular impediment when foreigners from European and western cultures come to work in animistically oriented societies to offer development aid, to get involved in NGOs, whether under secular government auspices or the church, as doctors, soldiers, engineers, lecturers, teachers, or in specifically Christian mission. This is because animism not only contains religious elements, but with its particular concept of the world and of man constitutes an all-embracing system of orienting oneself, serving that society as a way of shaping and coping with existence. One has to have some knowledge of this in order to understand the people among whom one is working and for one's work to have successful outcomes.

This textbook does not present animism from a European and western perspective but from that of the people who live it out. The sequence of the individual chapters is arranged in such a way that the reader can learn step by step what animism is, in order finally to understand those characteristic functions that belong to the medium and the shaman in animistic societies.

The author, a professor of ethnology, has considerable experience in this field. He has worked for five years in Oceania and has also undertaken numerous research expeditions in Africa, Asia and South America.

Pb. • pp. 284 • £ 22.50 • $ 37.50 • € 29.95
ISBN 978-3-95776-111-8

VTR Publications • Gogolstr. 33 • 90475 Nürnberg • Germany
info@vtr-online.com • http://www.vtr-online.com